Shigeru Uchida　　　内田 繁

Designscape　　　デザインスケープ

工作舎

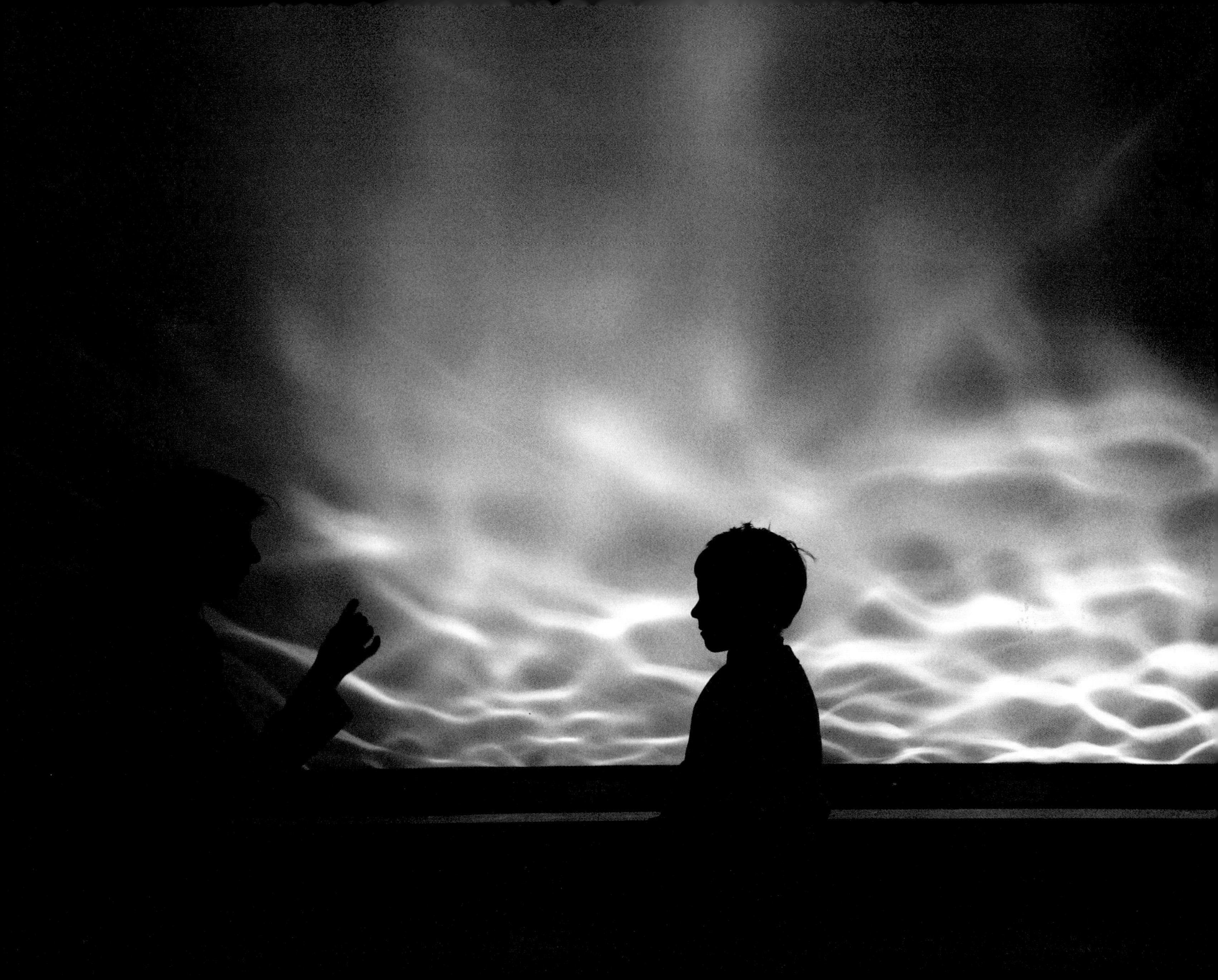

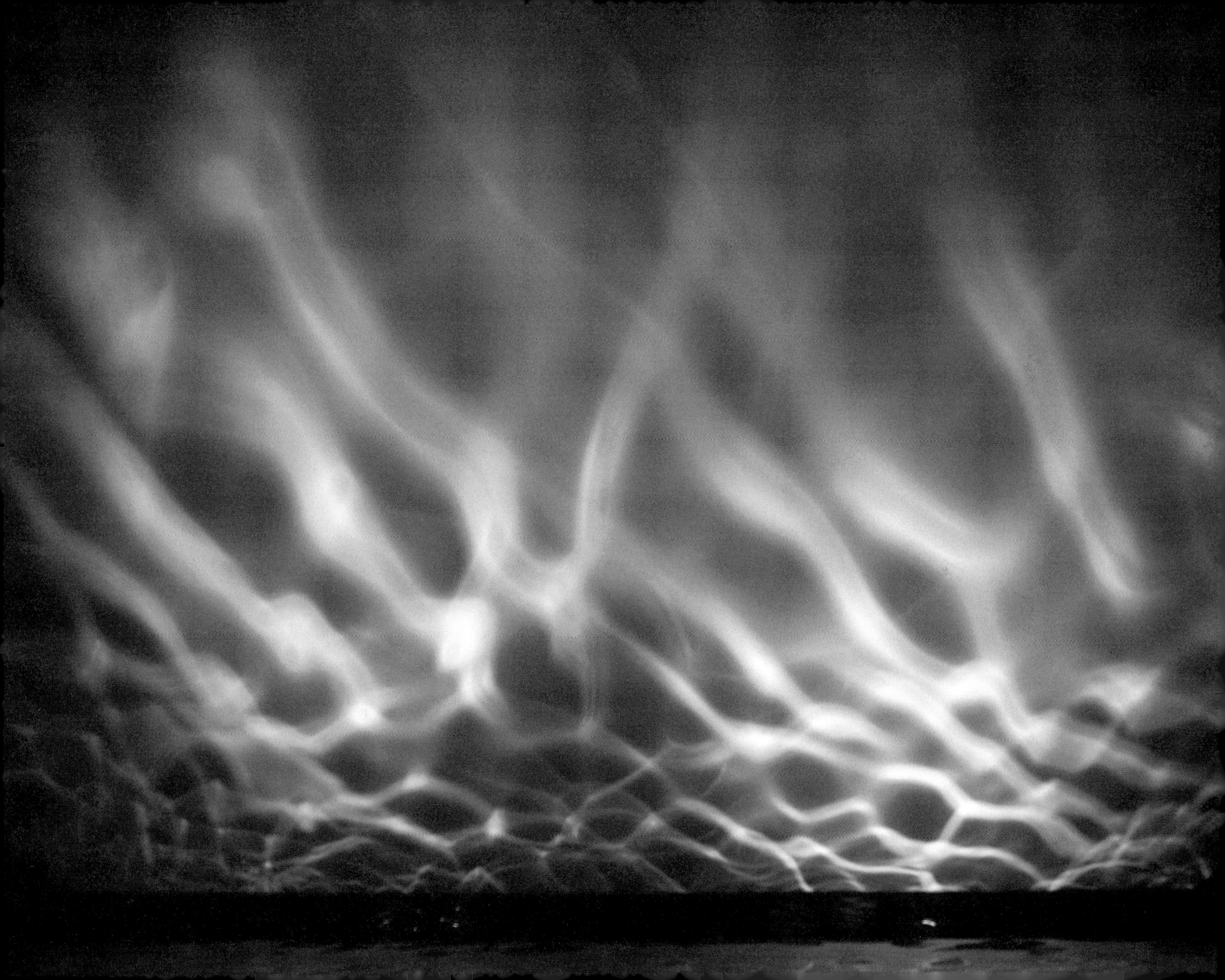

［変化の相］という日本の観念は、この世の一切のものは、変化し、生滅し、
常住したものは何もない、という［無常観］から生まれたものである。

変化の相とは、変化しないものは、いずれ朽ち果て死をむかえるという、
［変化こそ永遠である……］という観念を生み出す。
………そうした思考は［いま］という瞬間を際立たせる。

［いま］とは、過去と未来の中間にあるいまを言うのではなく、
［いま］瞬間にこそ過去も未来もすべてがあるといった観念である。

［無常観］はやがて［無情美観］へと転化する。
……［わび］である。

日本の美は［無情］という、はかなく、わびしく、さみしく、心細い、
消極的な境地を心理的な美として転化し、積極的な価値を見いだす。
……幽玄、閑寂な境地である。

The Japanese concept of transience arose out of a perception of the evanescence of life,
the realization that nothing in this world is permanent,
everything changes, and everything that is born must also die.

The notion of transience in turn leads to the idea that "only change itself is perpetual" :
things that do not change will sooner or later fade away and die.
In this line of thought, the present moment - "now" - is highly conspicuous.

"Now" is not the interval between the past and the future;
"Now" is the moment that includes both the past and the future.

In due time, the view of life as transient
and empty led to the harsh kind of esthetics called *wabi*.

The Japanese sense of beauty transforms a heartless and negative state of fleetingness,
cheerlessness, sadness and loneliness into something psychologically beautiful and positive,
a state of mysterious profundity and tranquility.

01

花の色は雪にまじりて見えずともかをだににほへ人の知るべく
小野篁

Men cannot see the color of the blossoms,
a color mingled now with snow,
but only let them breathe the fragrance,
and all must know the plum trees are in flower.
Ono no Takamura

我々にとっての「夏」は、虫の音がすでに秋を含み、
はずした障子が冬の風を含んでいる夏である。
和辻哲郎

For us, "summer" already contains the autumn in the sounds of the insects,
and the winter wind in the removed paper doors.
Tetsuro Watsuji

現在ただいまを重ねることによって、すべてができあがってくる、
過去と未来をつなげないという考え方が日本には強いと思います。
内田 繁

I think the Japanese have a strong tendency to avoid linking the past and the future.
Everything is built up through an accumulation of present moments.
Shigeru Uchida

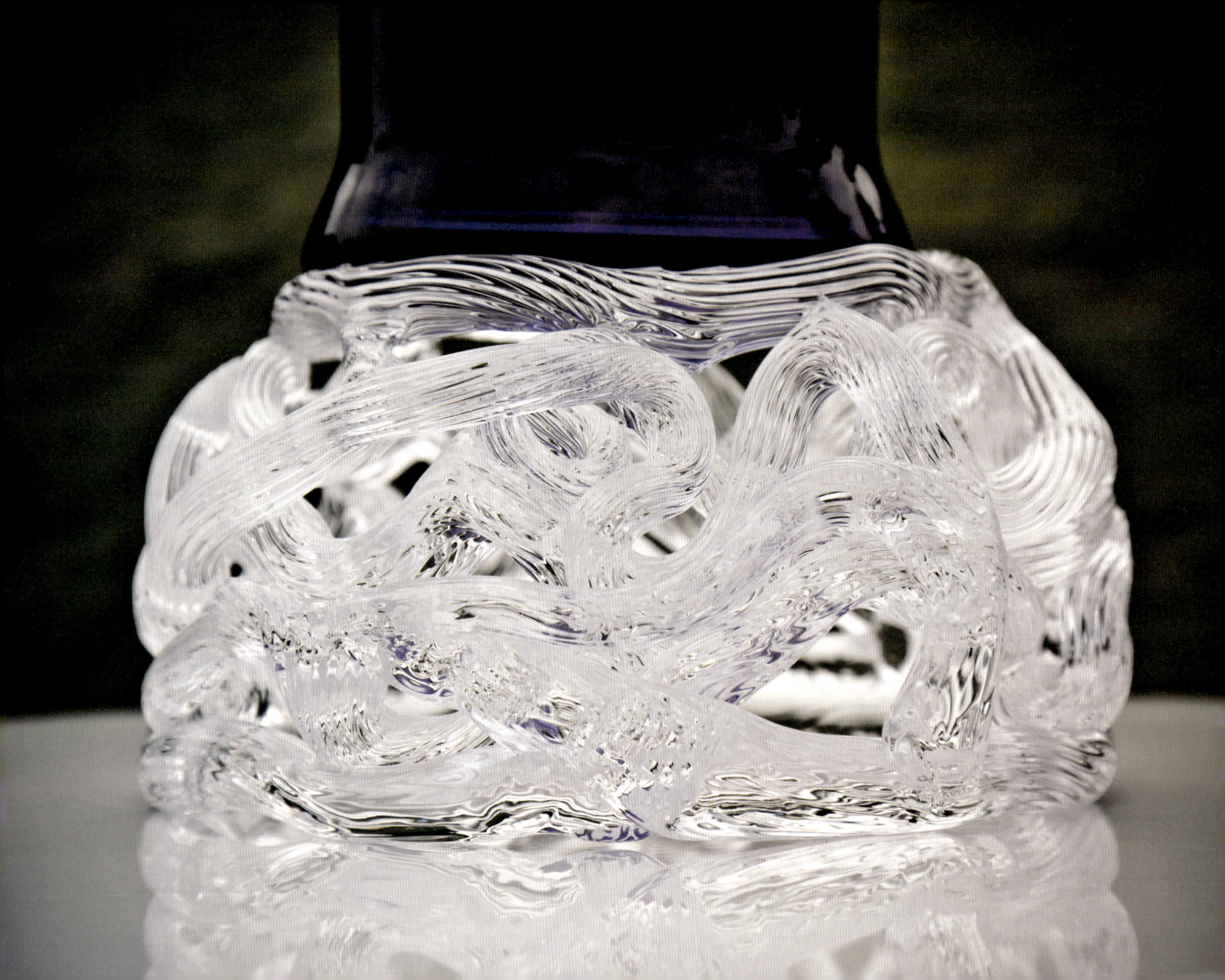

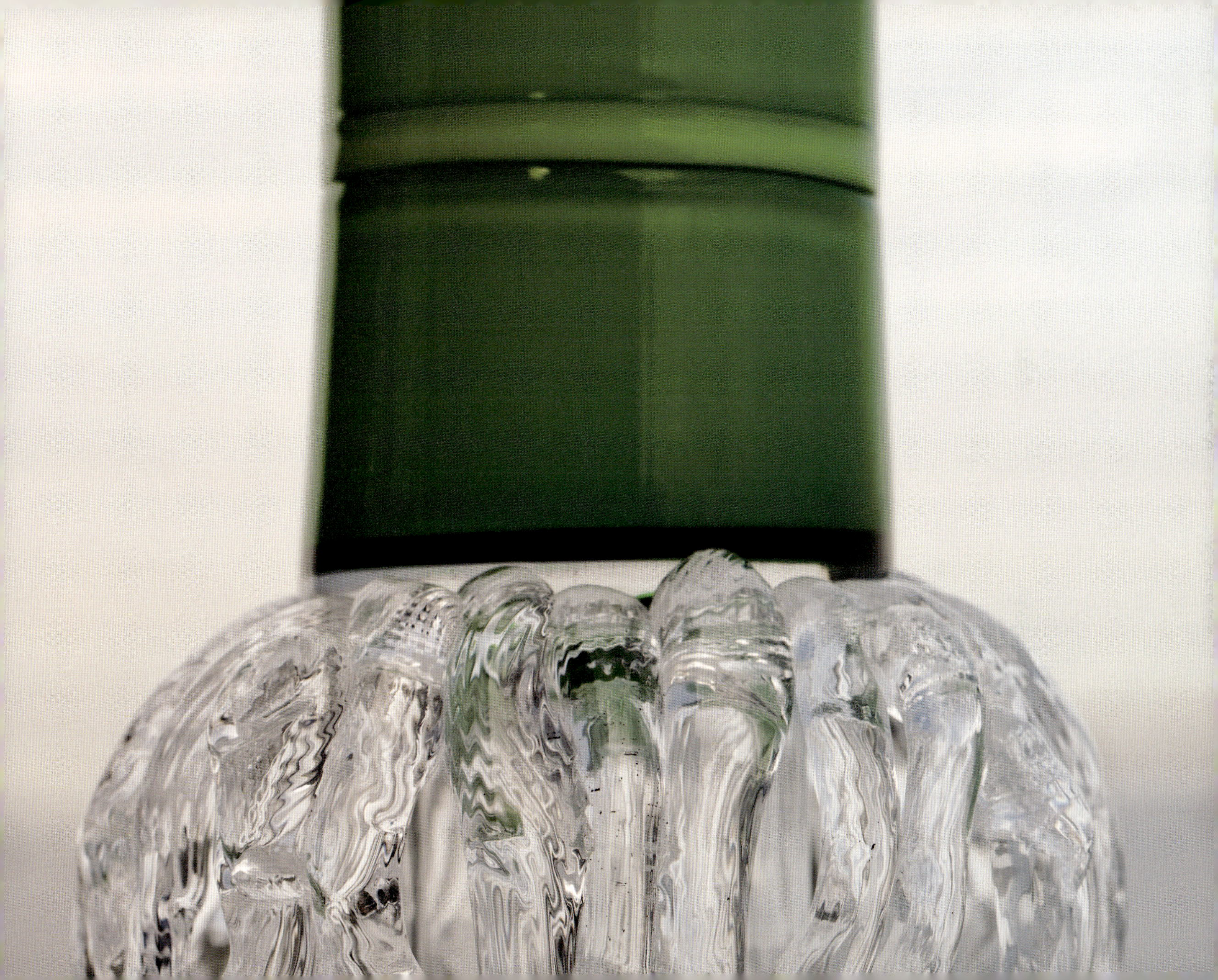

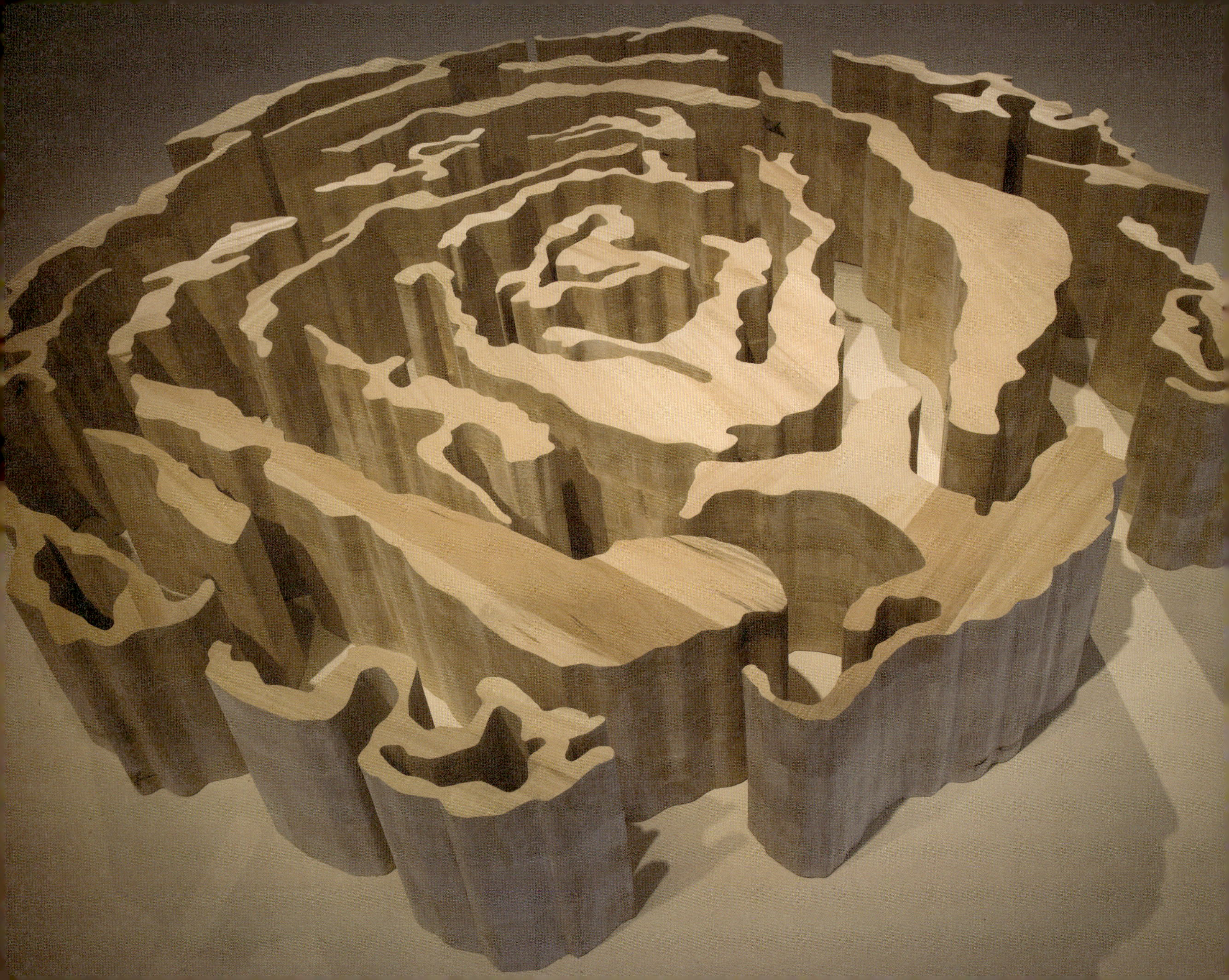

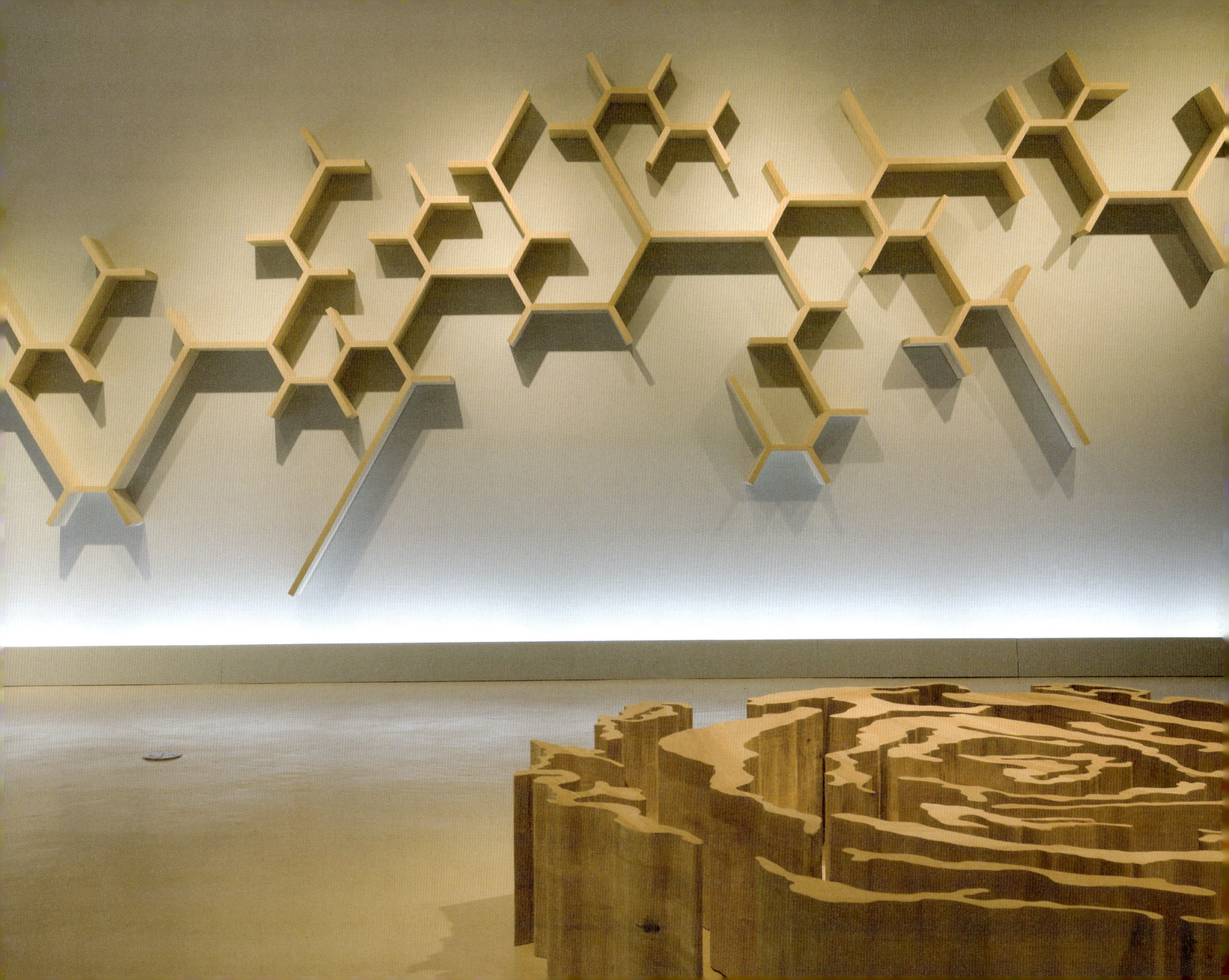

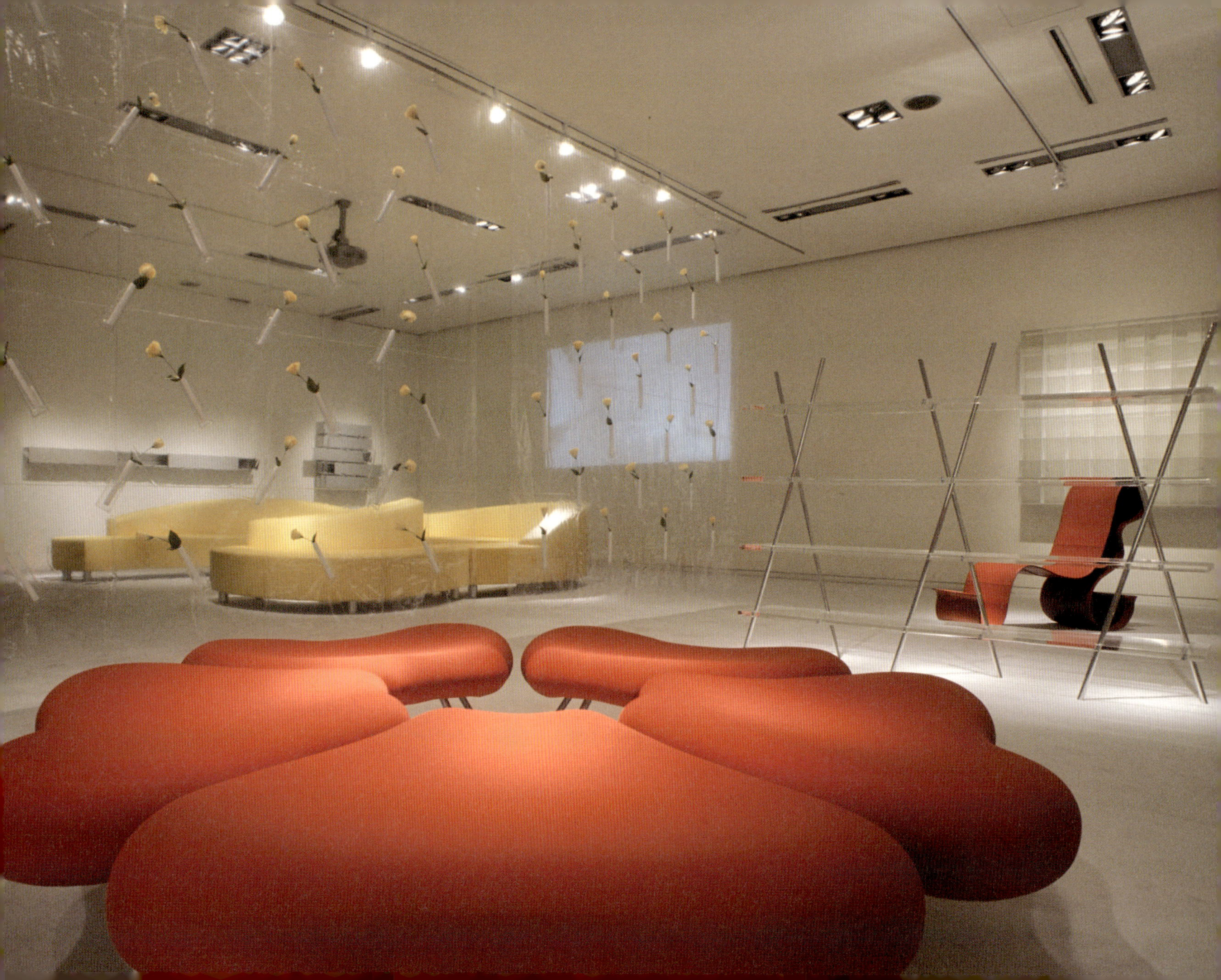

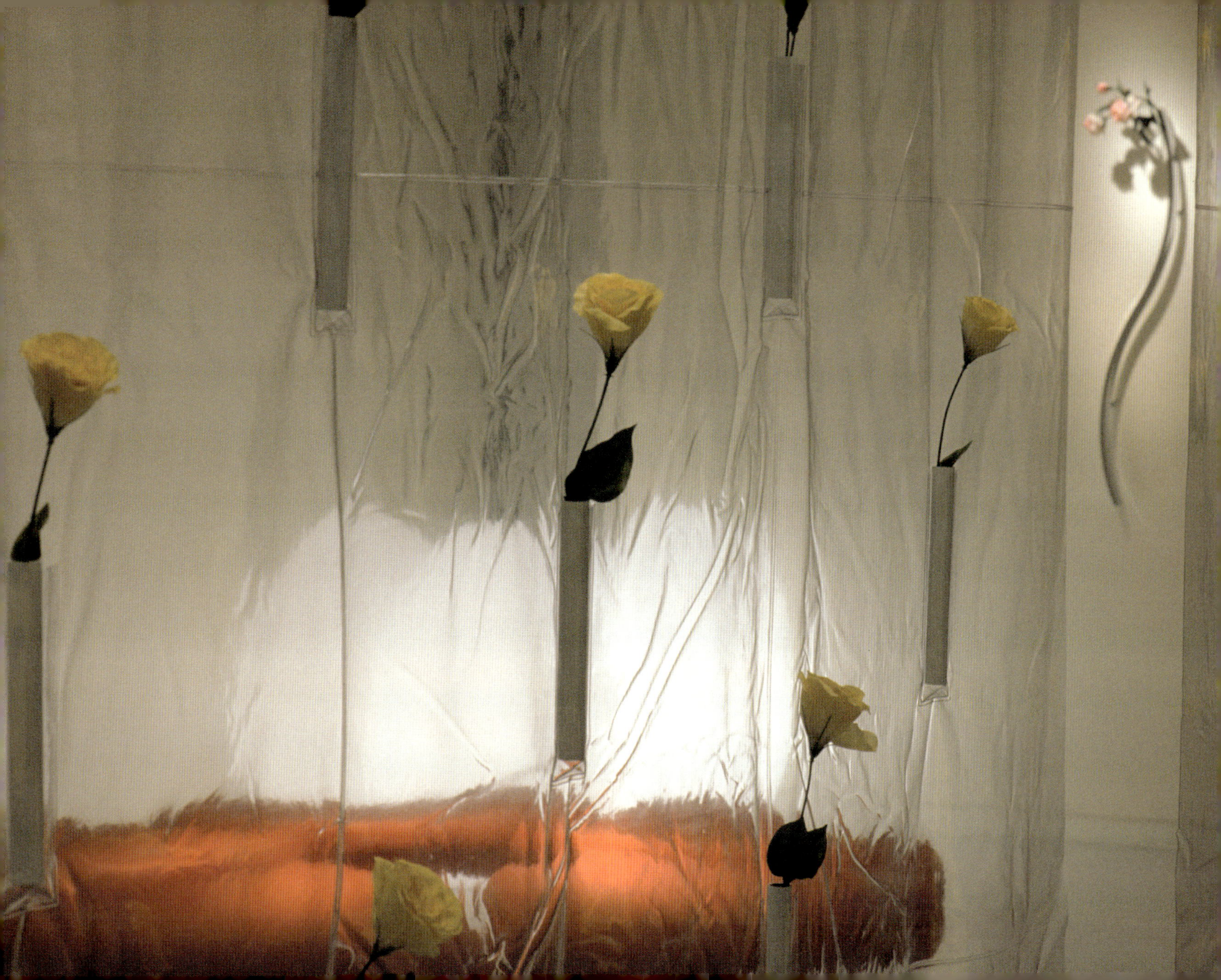

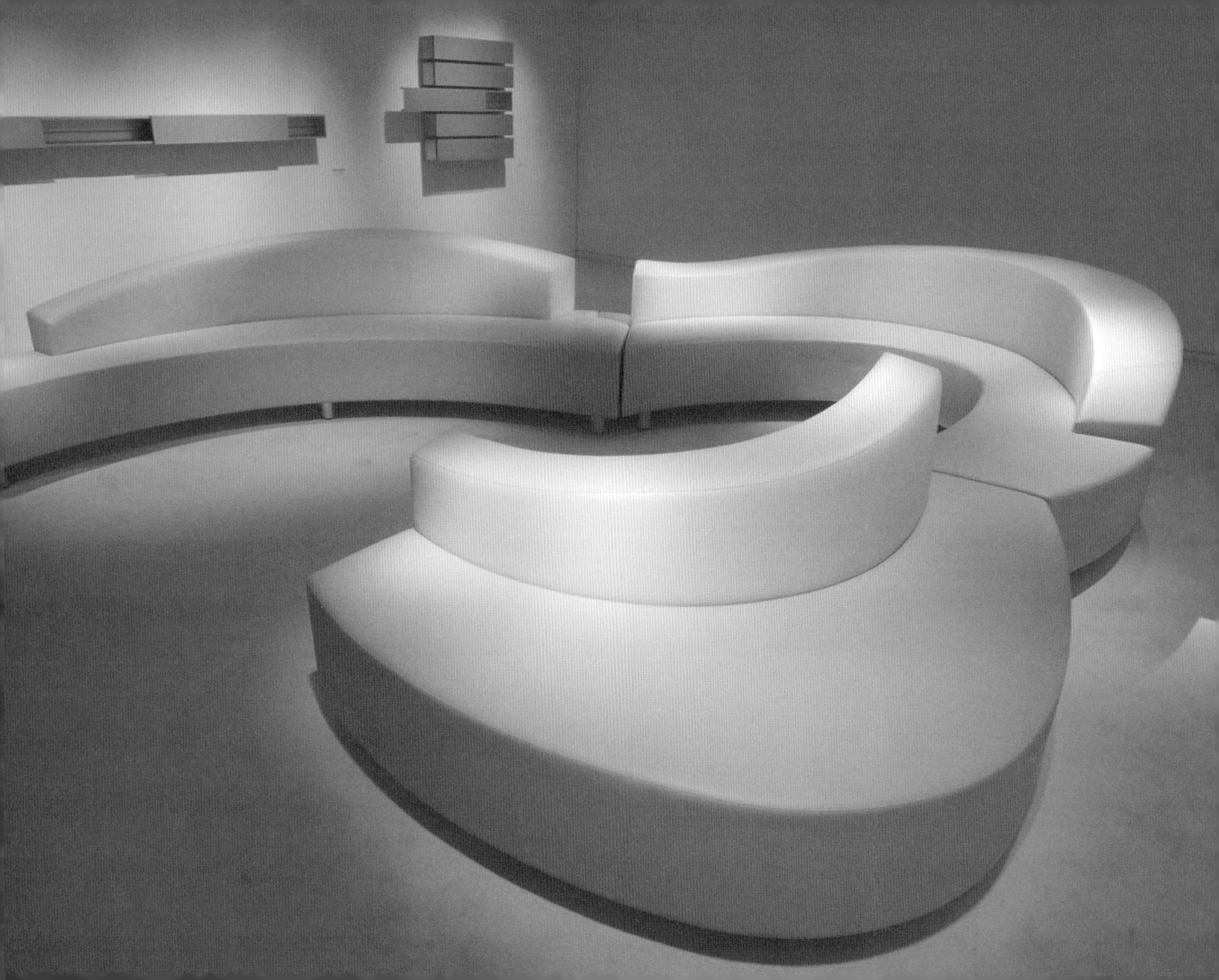

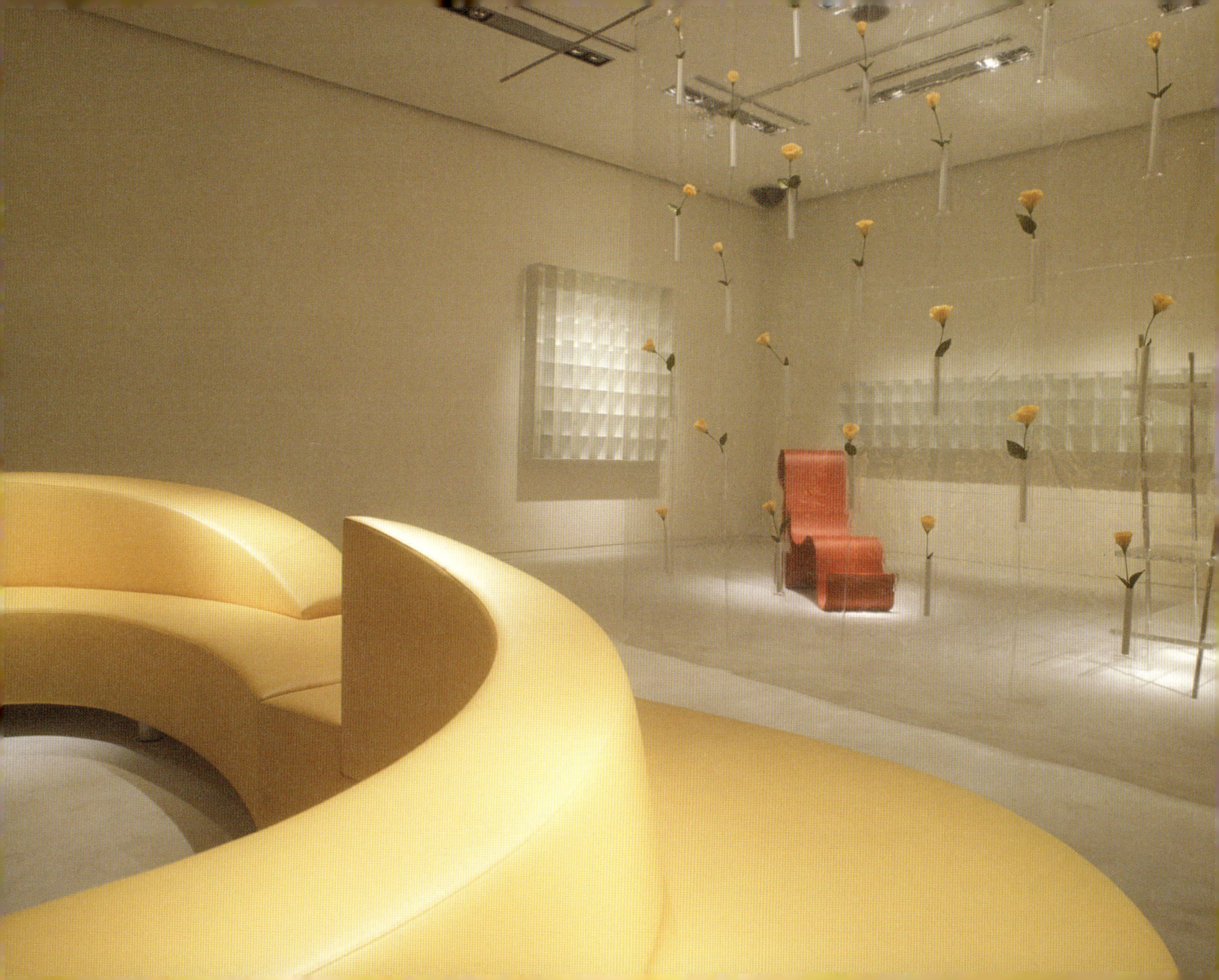

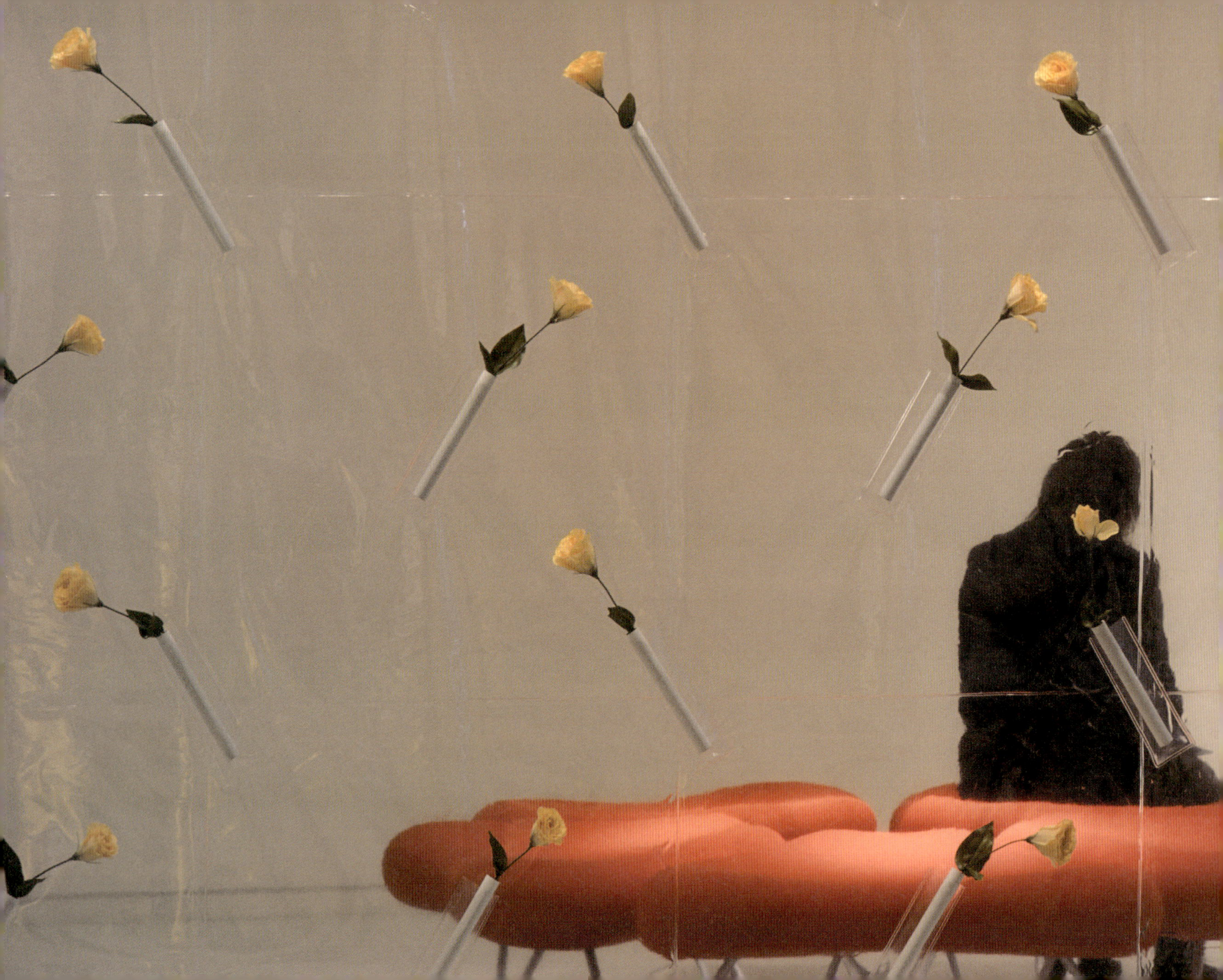

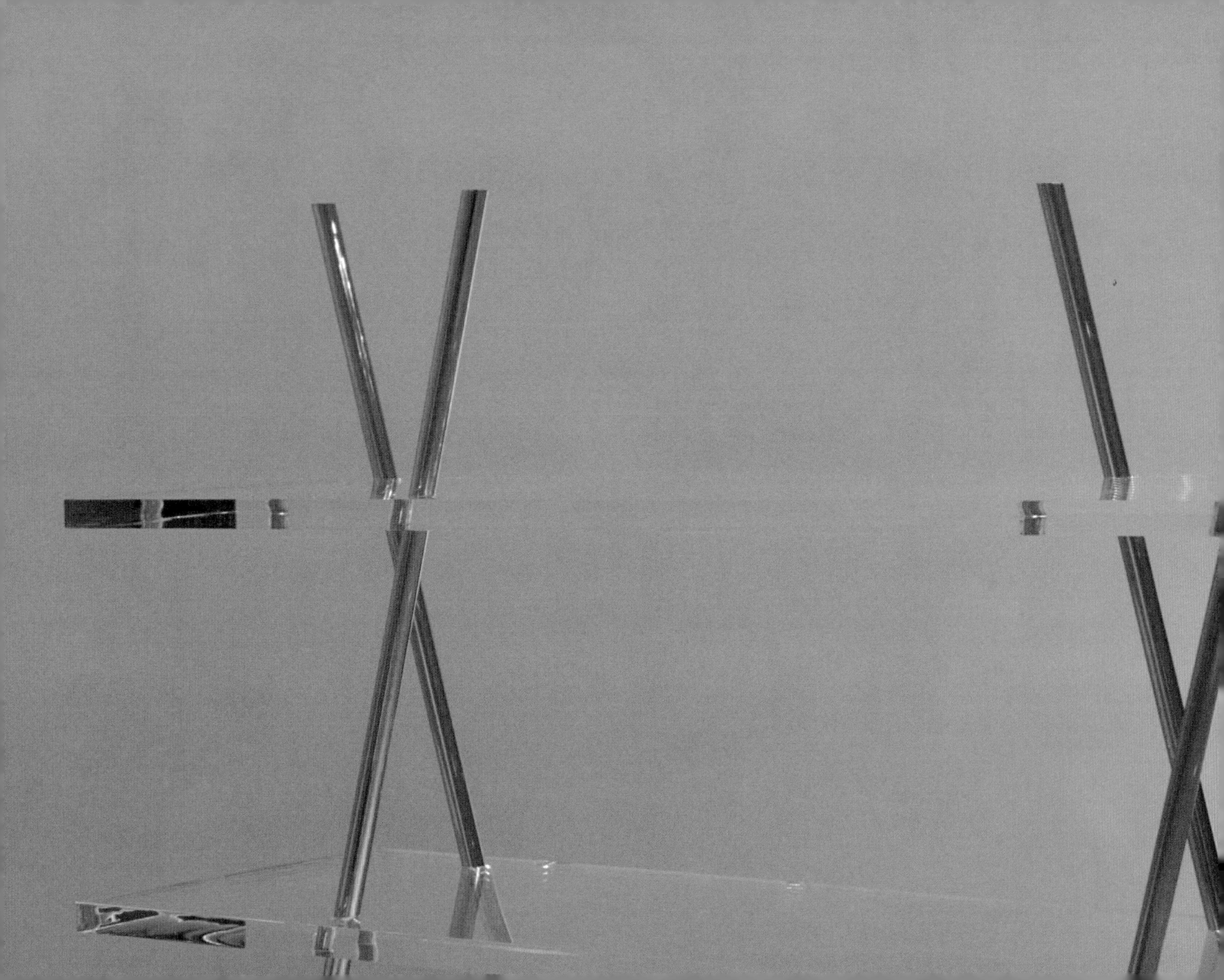

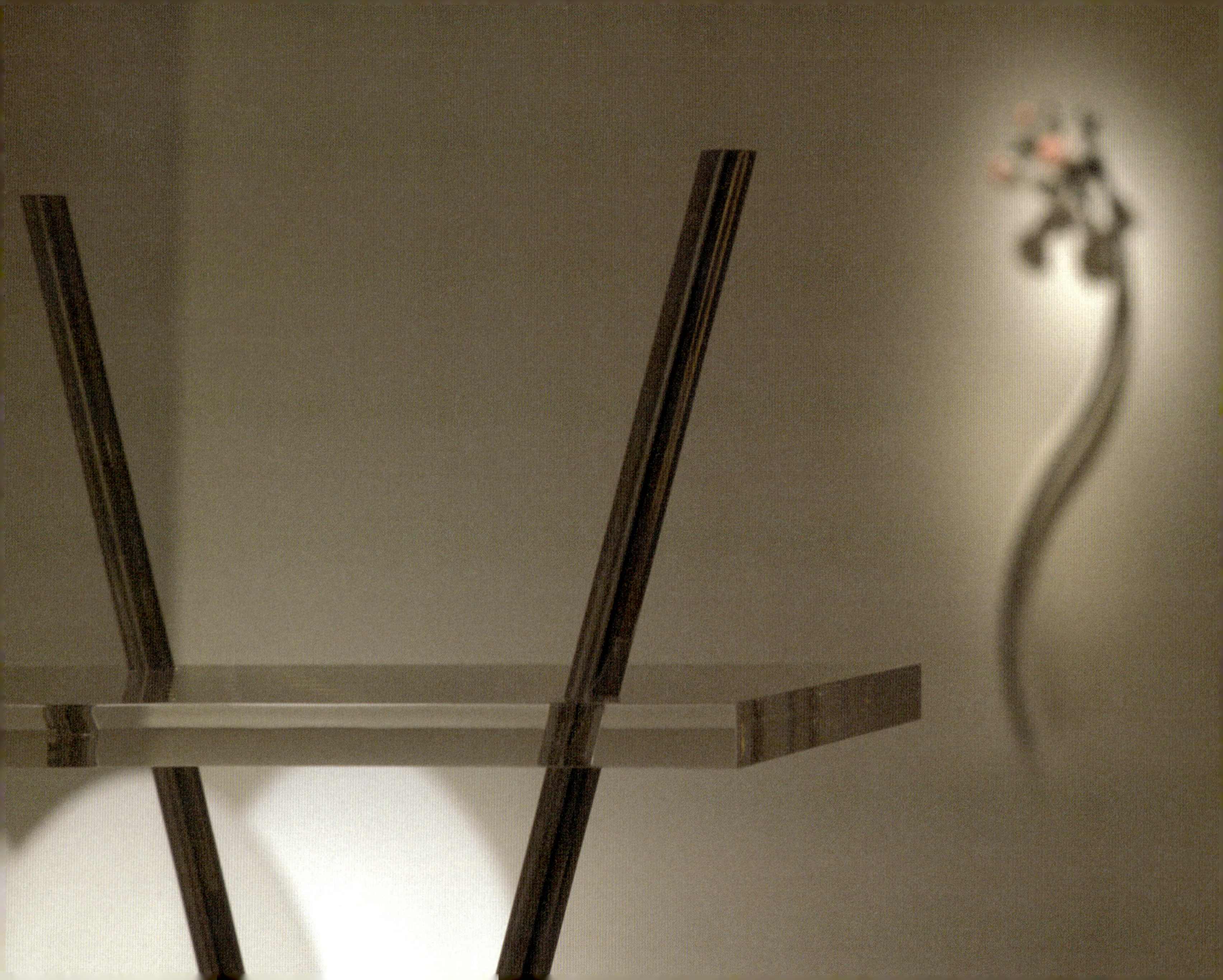

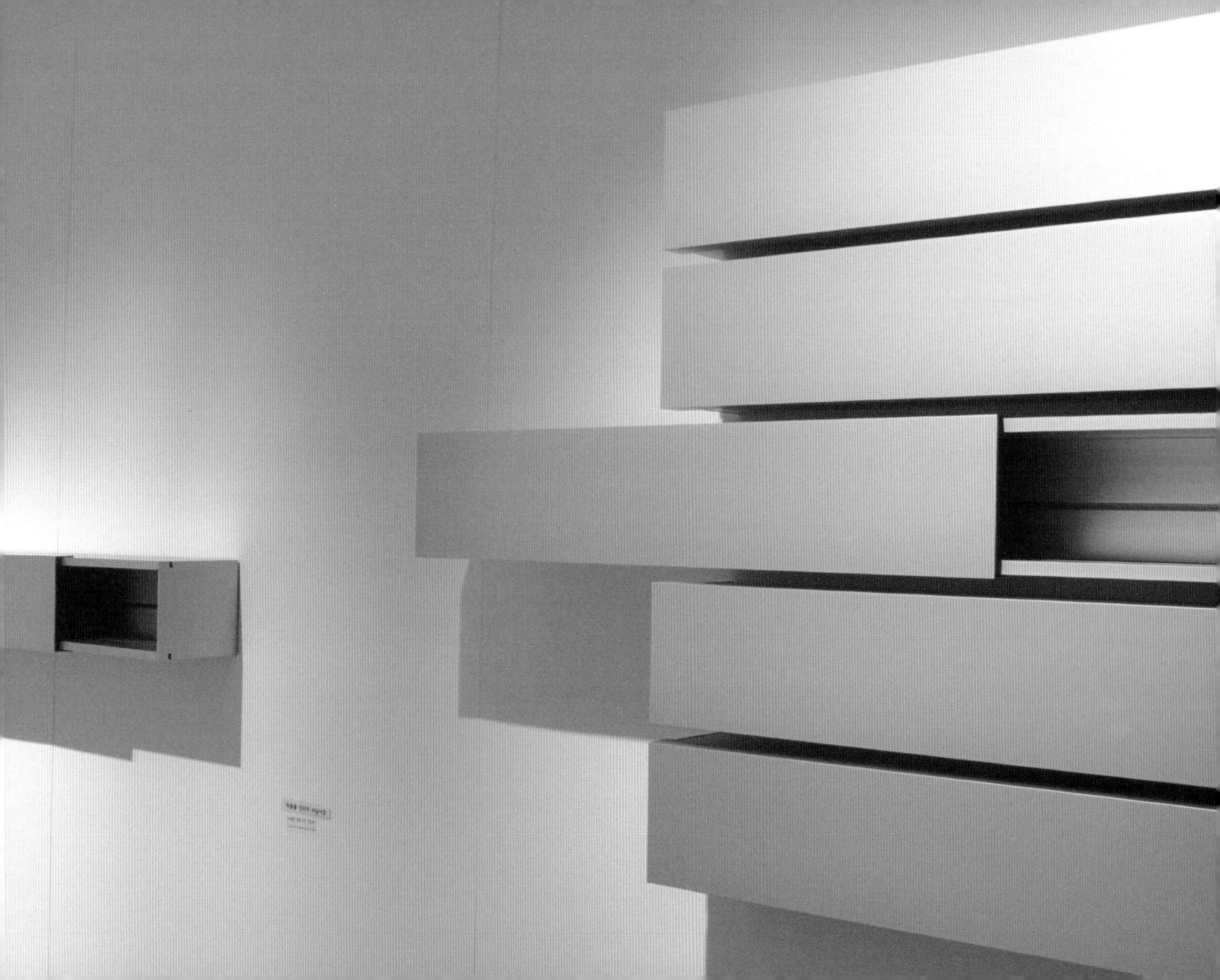

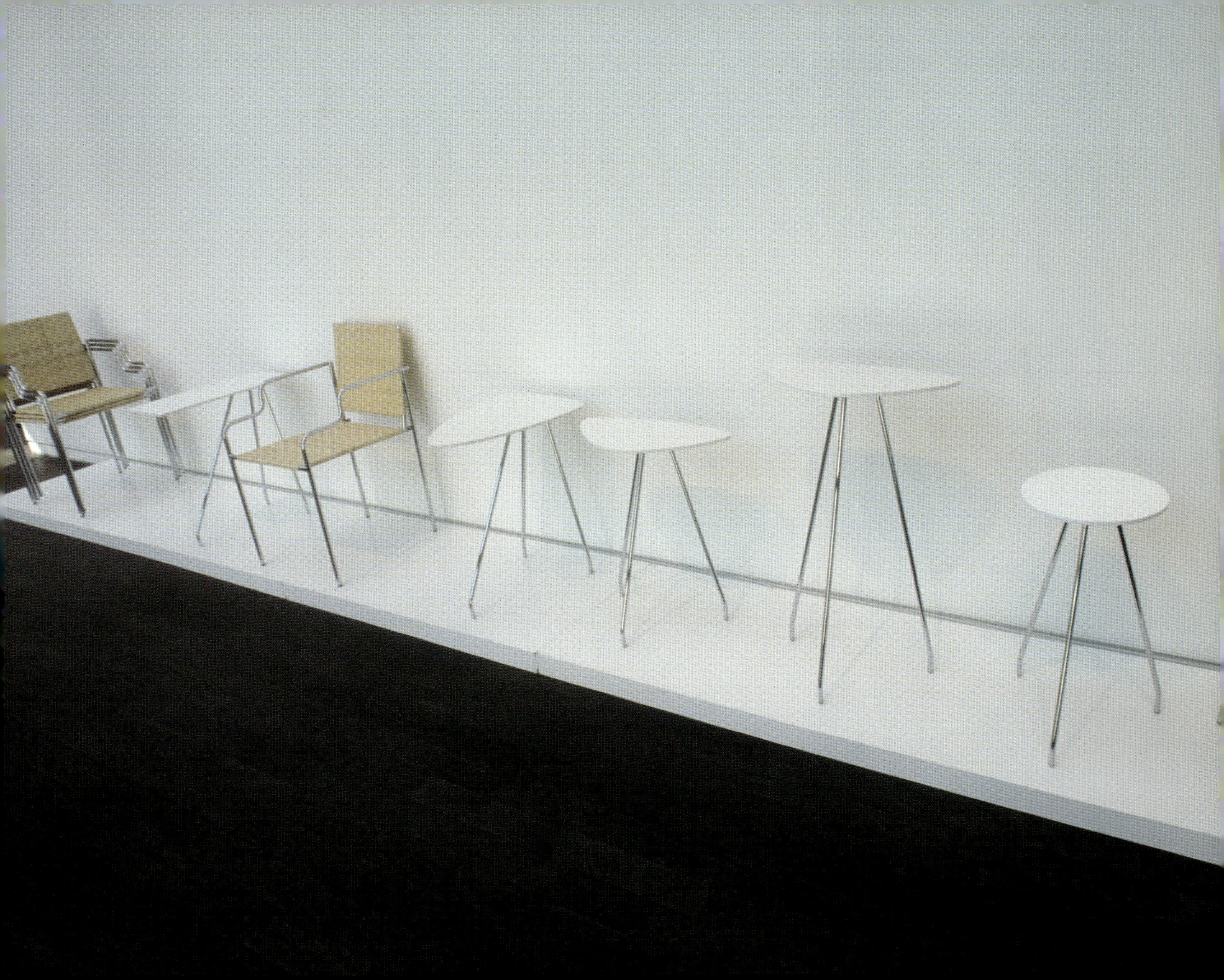

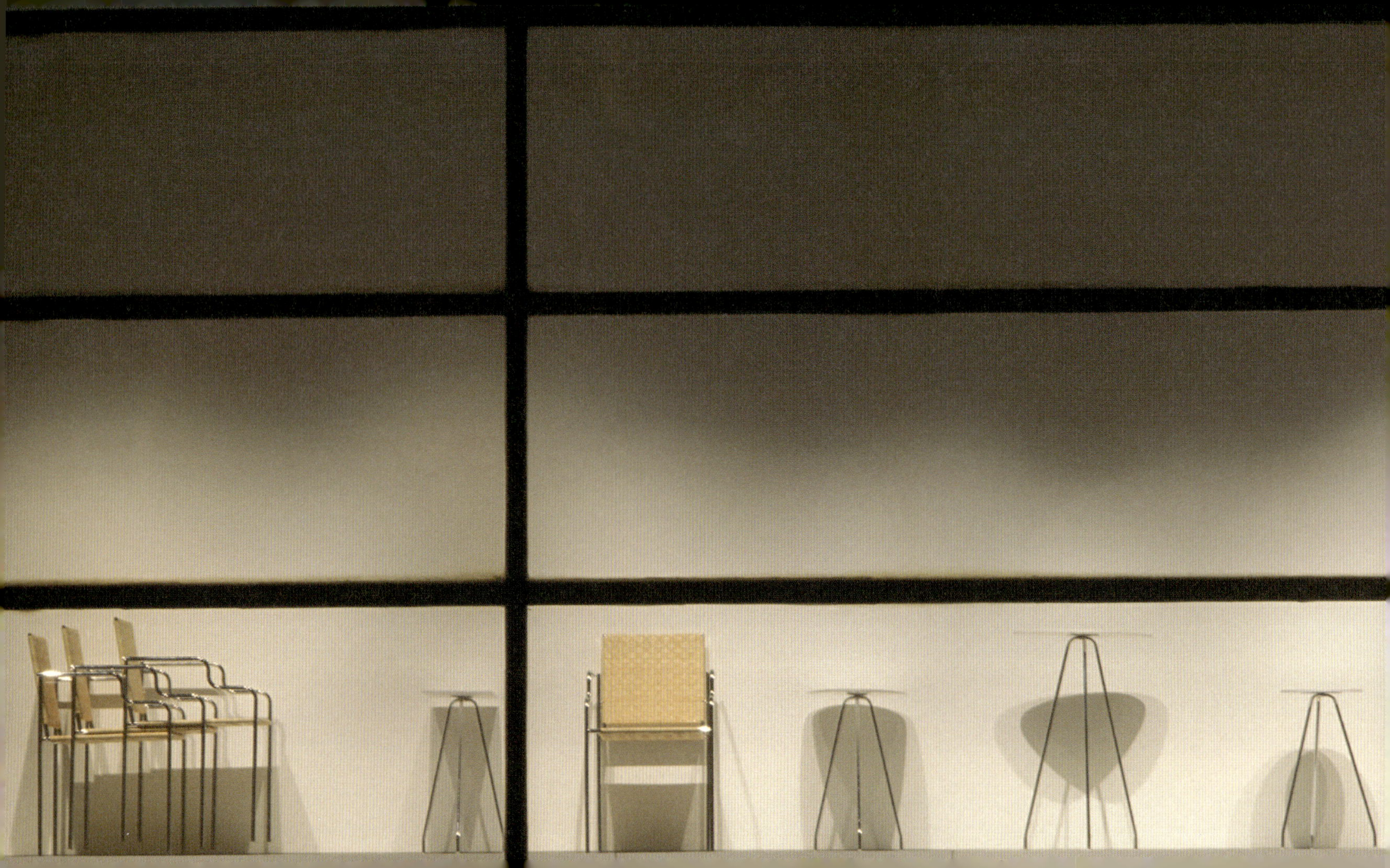

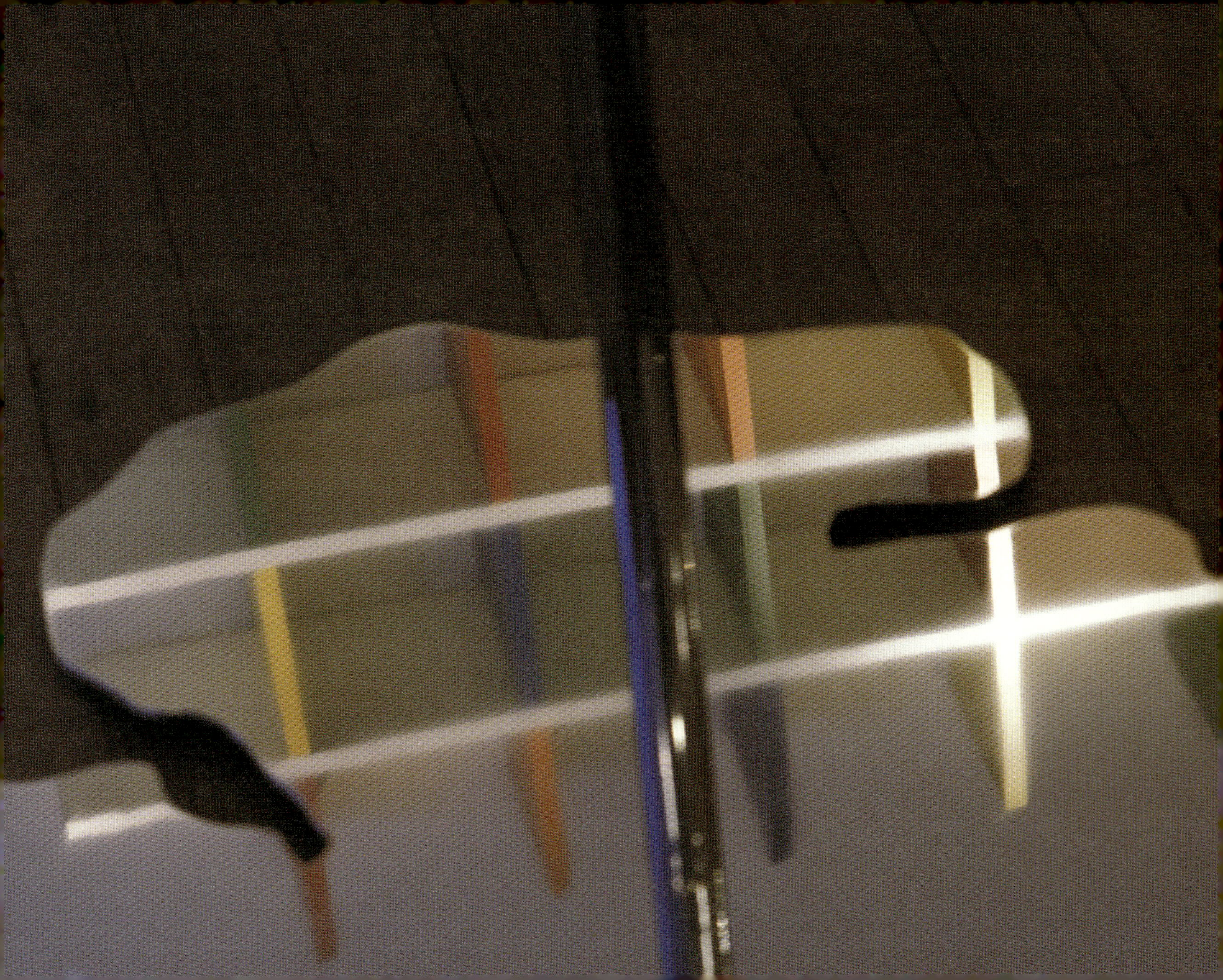

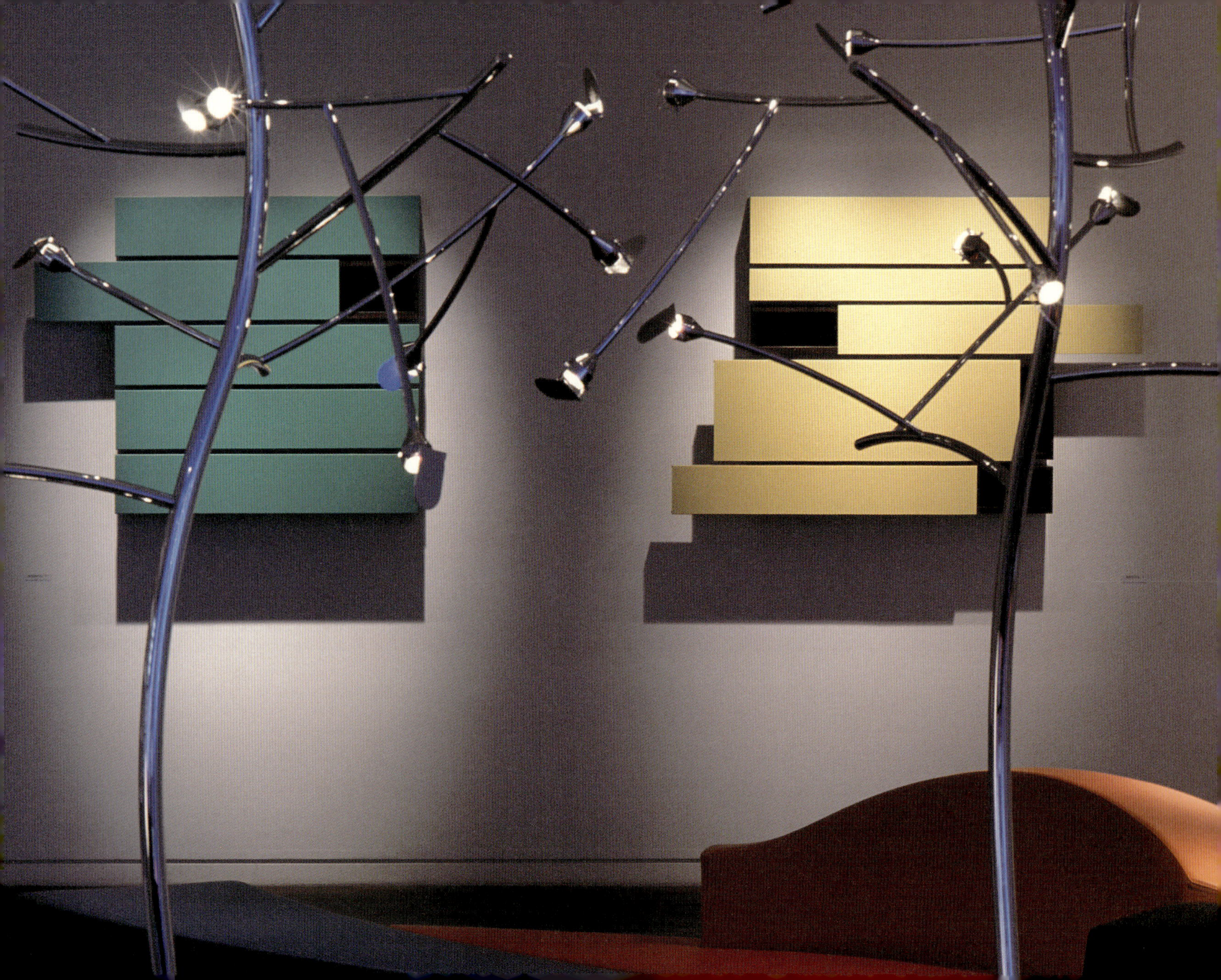

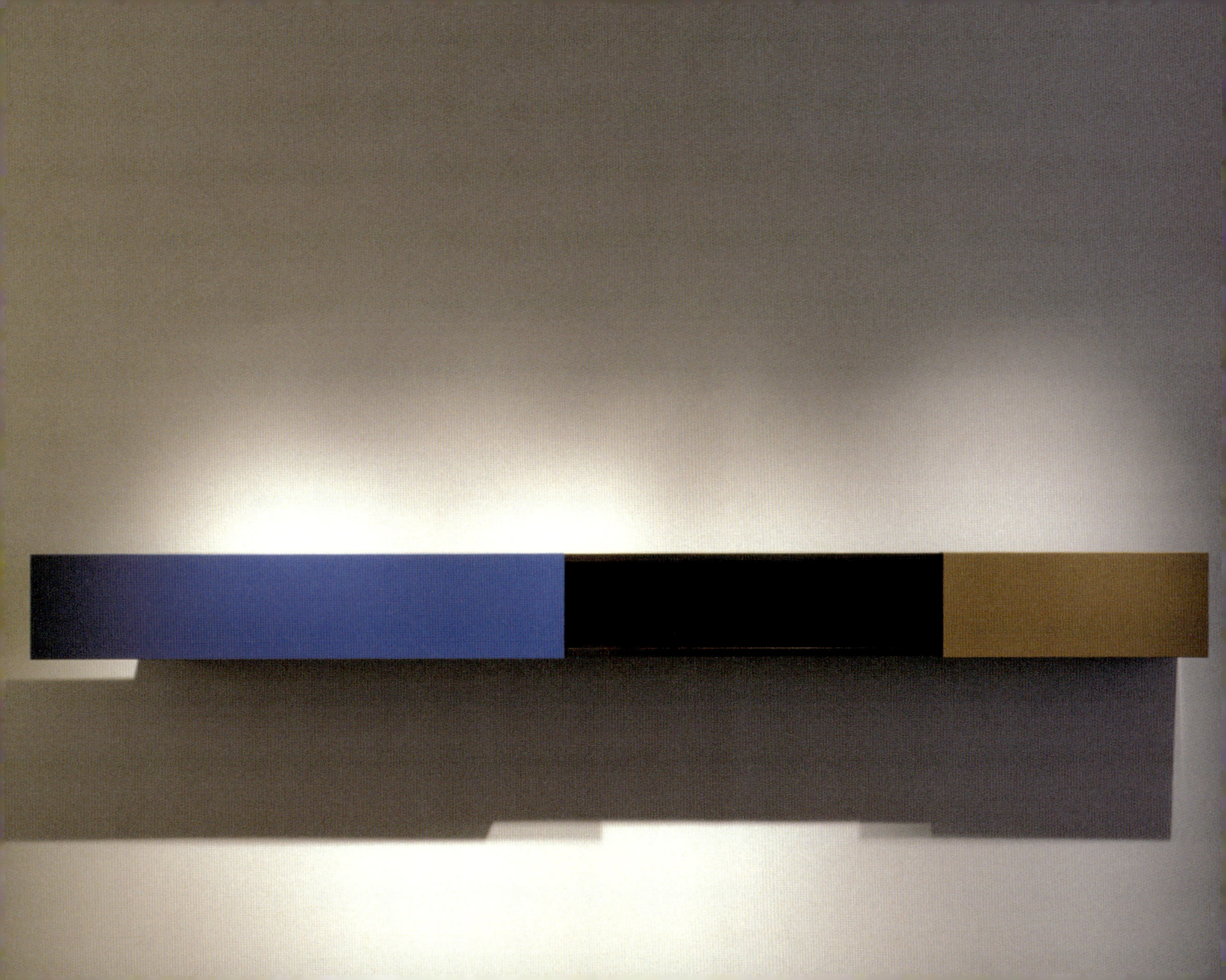

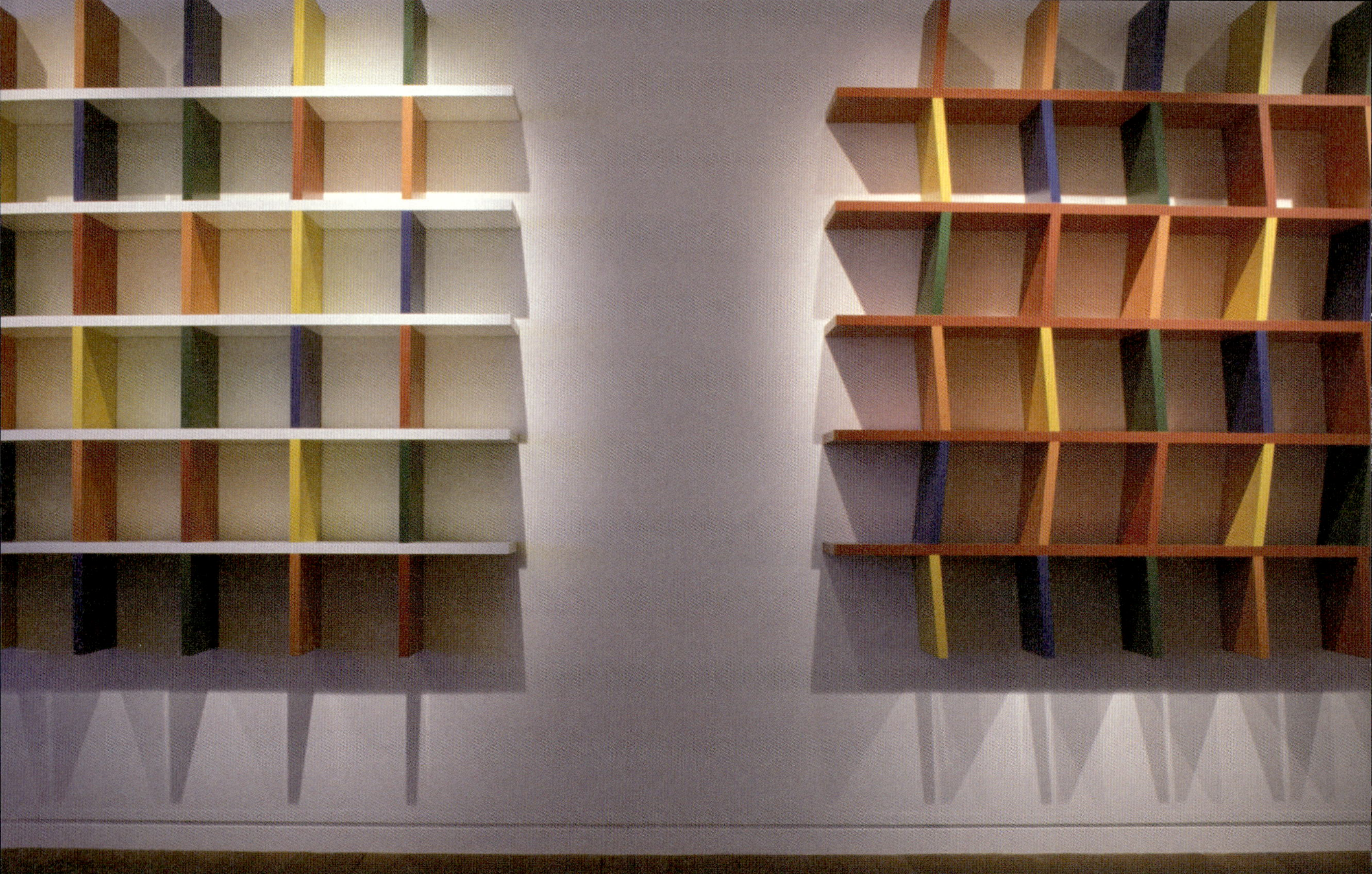

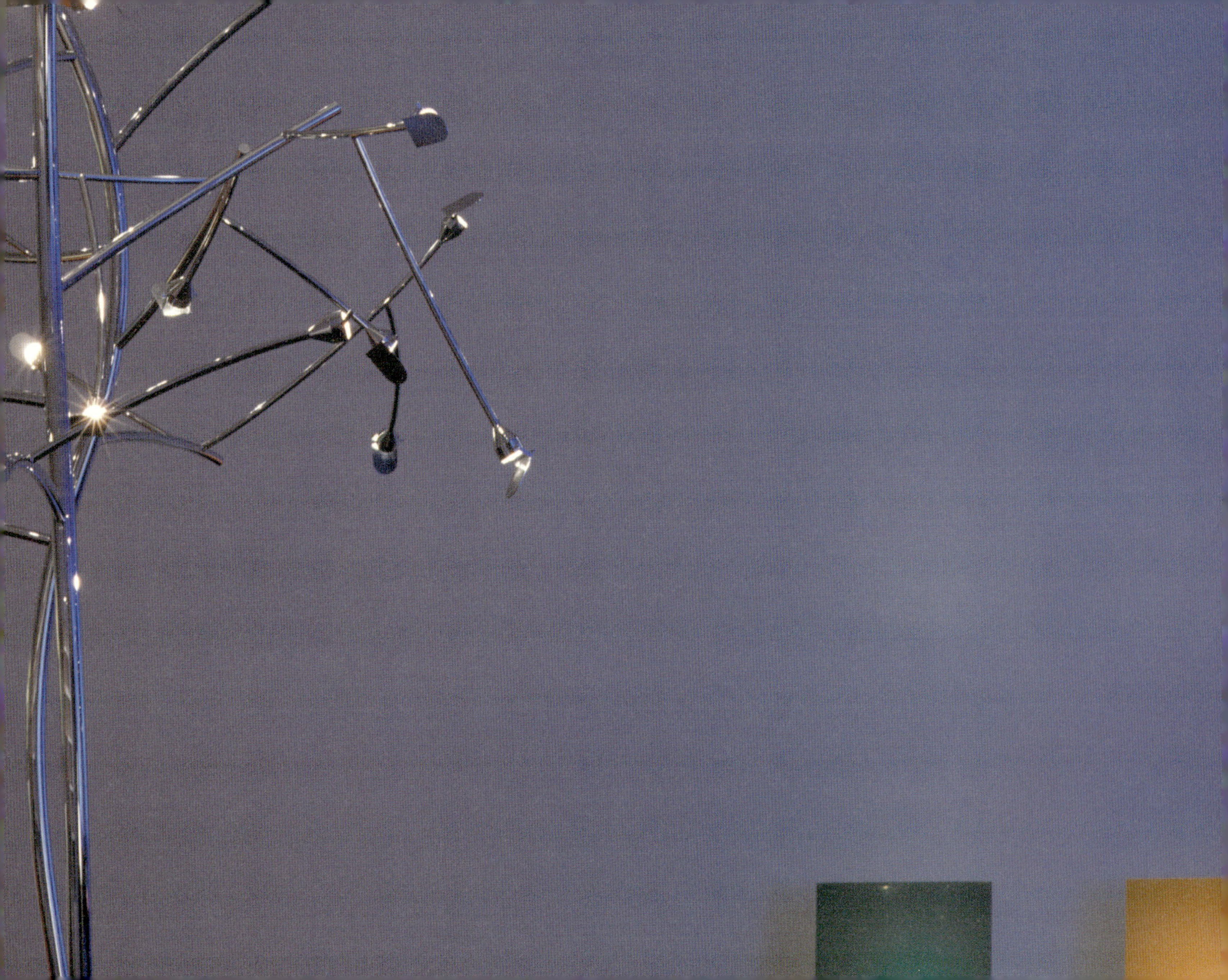

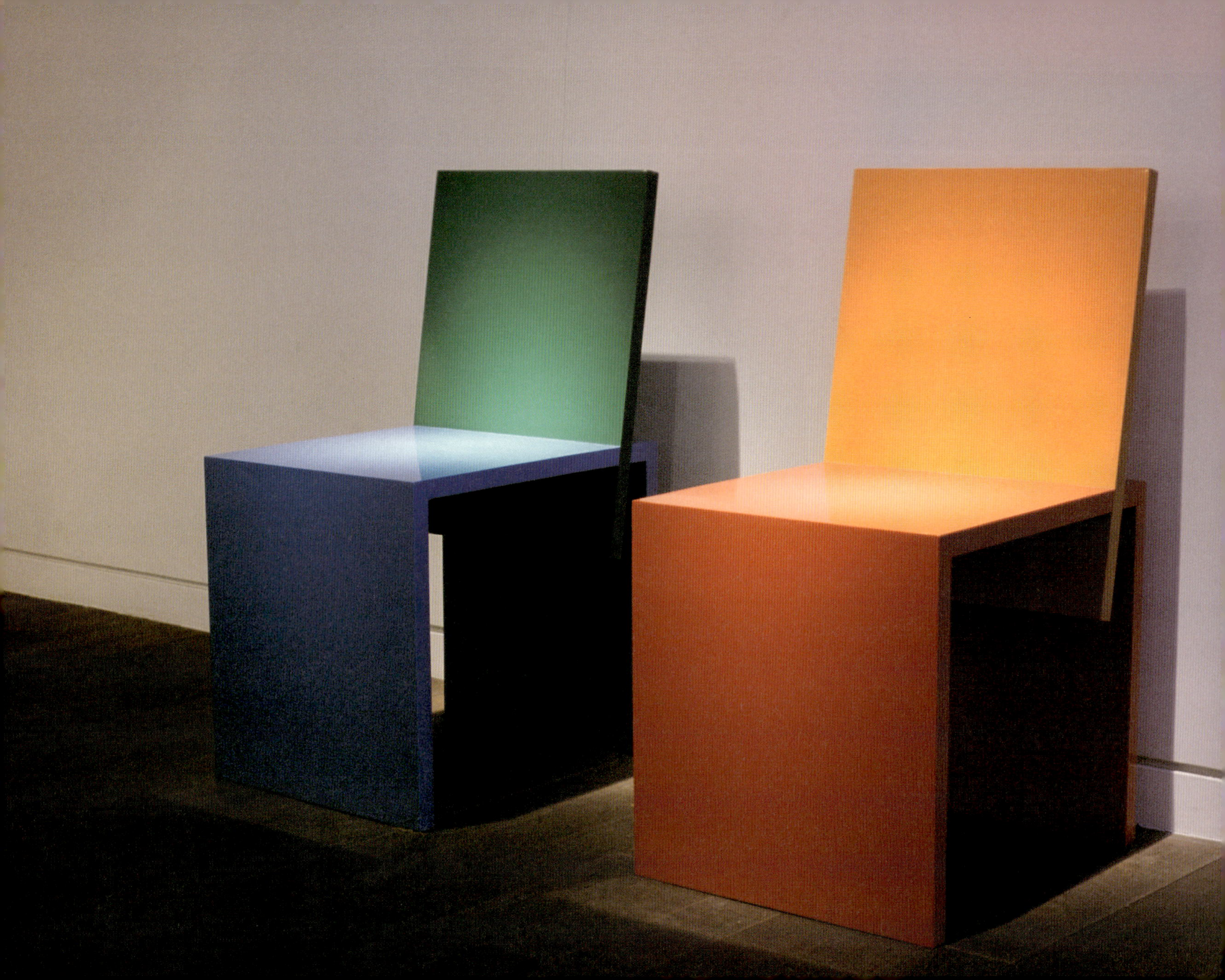

02

月影ゆかしくは、南面に池を掘れ、
さてぞ見る、琴(きん)のことの音ききたくば、
北の岡の上に松を植えよ。
「梁塵秘抄」

To enjoy the moonlight,
dig a pond and take a look.
To hear the sound of the koto,
plant some pines and listen to the wind.
(Ryojin Hisho)

われわれは、一本の敷居だけで、
そこから違う空間がはじまることを了解できます。
内田 繁

We realize that a different space begins just on the other side of the threshold.
Shigeru Uchida

神の住居、聖なる家は永遠ではない。
むしろ必ず亡び、また復活するものである。
吉田光邦

The houses of the gods and other sacred buildings are not eternal.
On the contrary, they are invariably ruined but are always resurrected.
Mitsukuni Yoshida

Discovery of Stillness

This piece represents Uchida's works from 1970 to the late 1980's. The thin pipe and chair legs painted black were ahead of the various images adopted by many other artists. The most representative art works in this period was 'September' (1977), which became a permanent collection at the Metropolitan Museum of Art. Transparency and liveliness of the thin black pipe, stainless mesh chair, etc, continues to the 'Discovery of Stillness'. During this period, Uchida continues to experience the 'Space of Nothingness' and 'Discovery of Stillness'.

Uchida said black and white present a pure form, which do not affected by others, and, delicate expression delivers kindness and delicateness, distress and frustration, which is unlike to harsh expression. Experience of 'Space of Nothingness' and 'Discovering of Stillness' brought Uchida to continue the ideology of weak modernity after 2000.

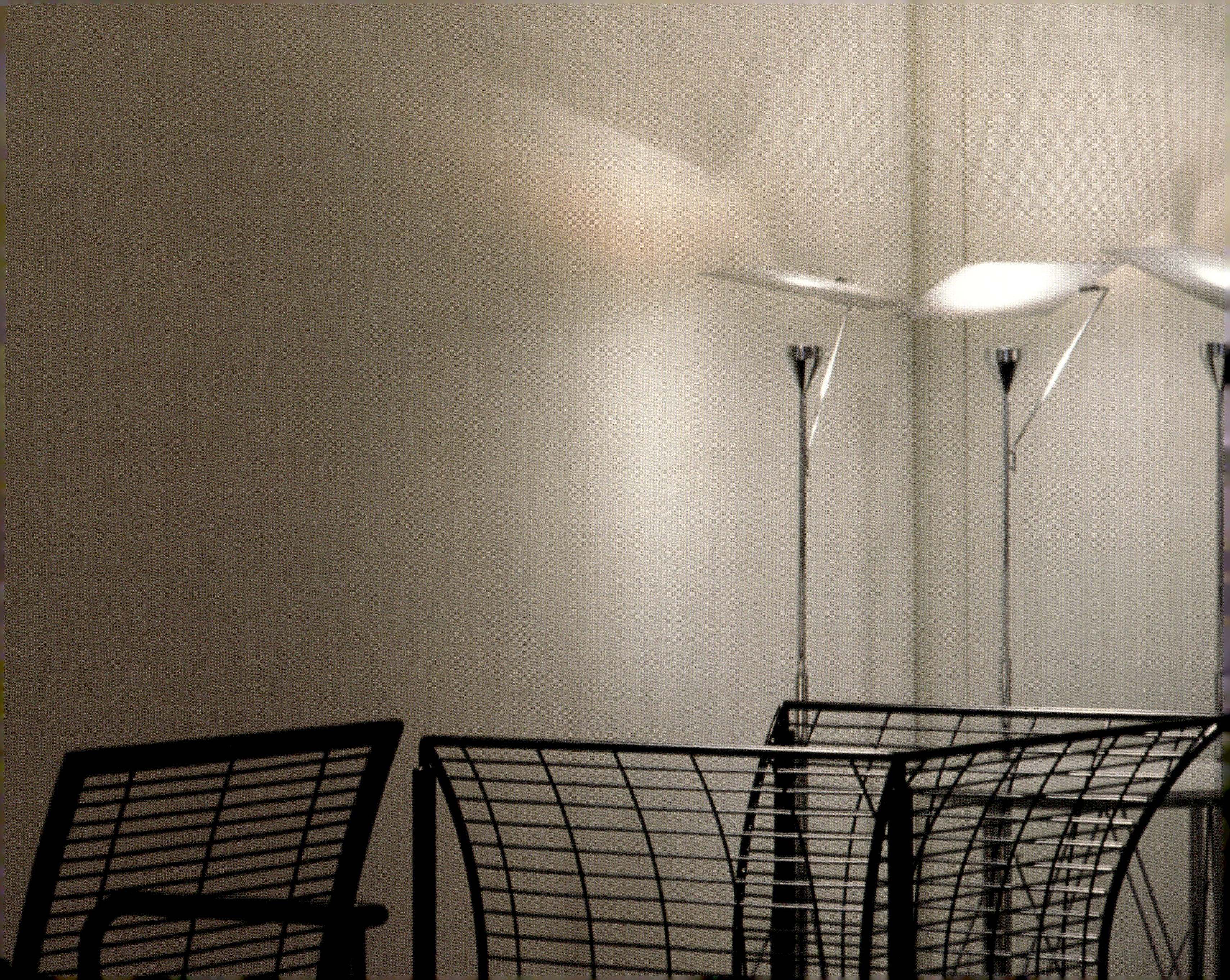

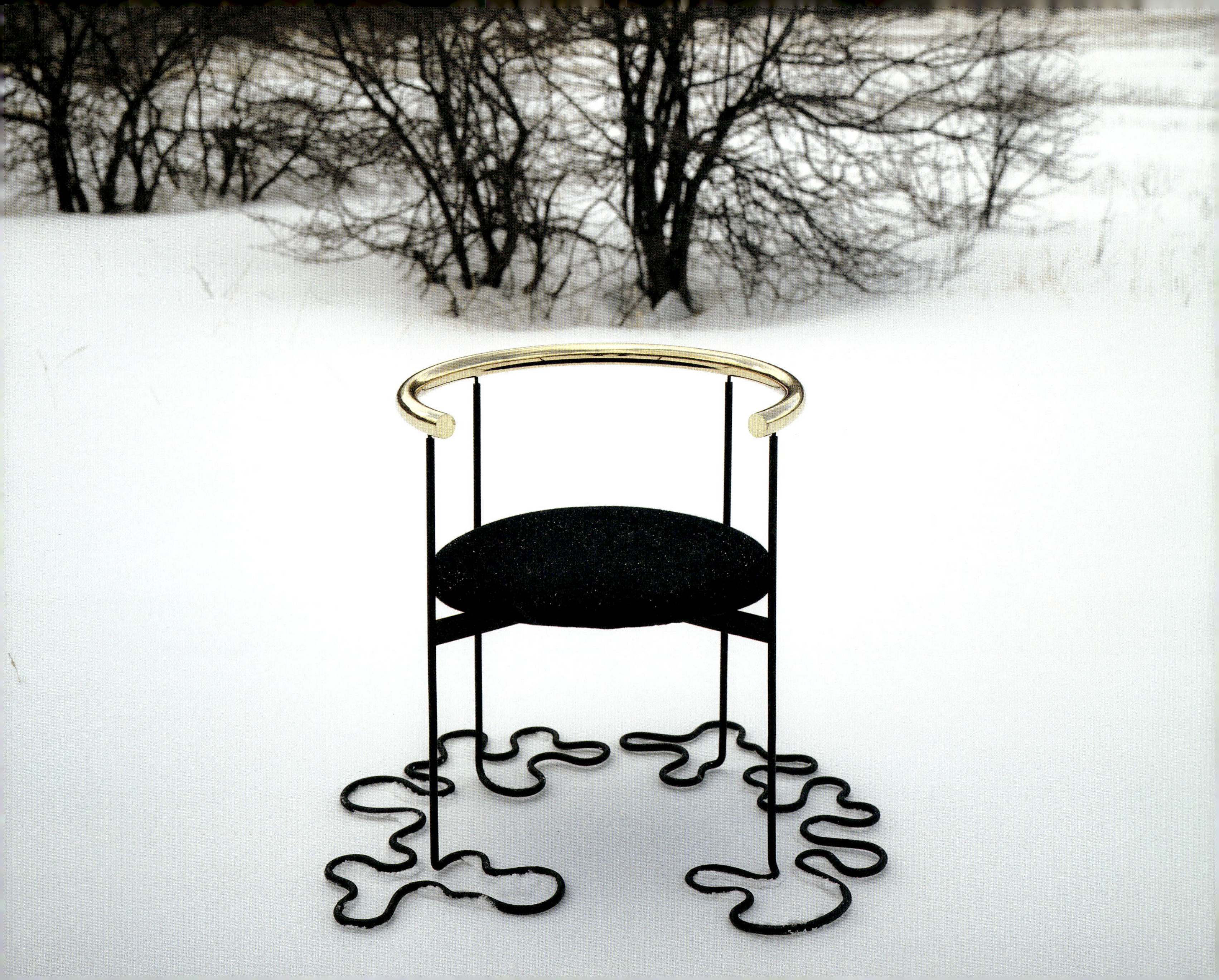

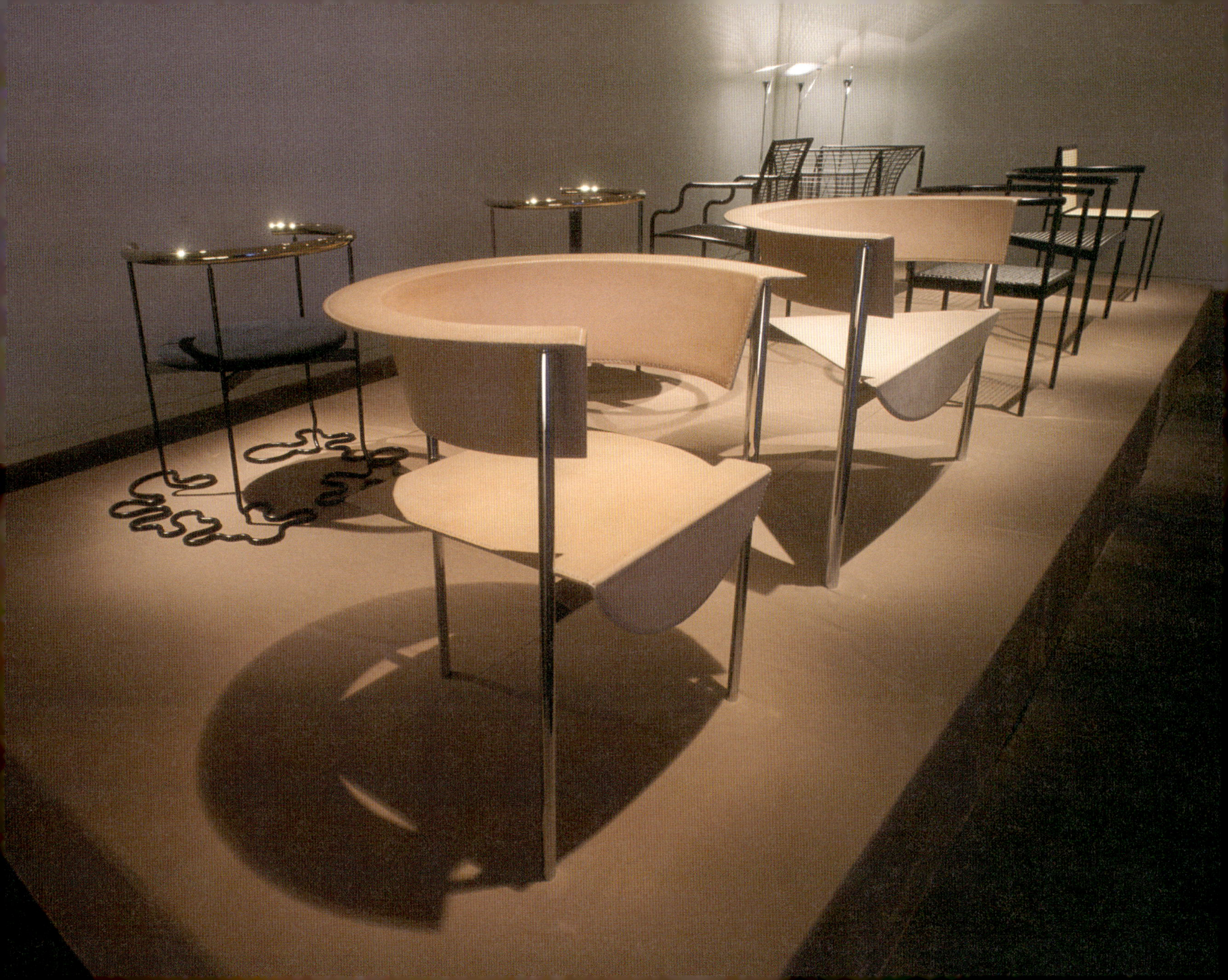

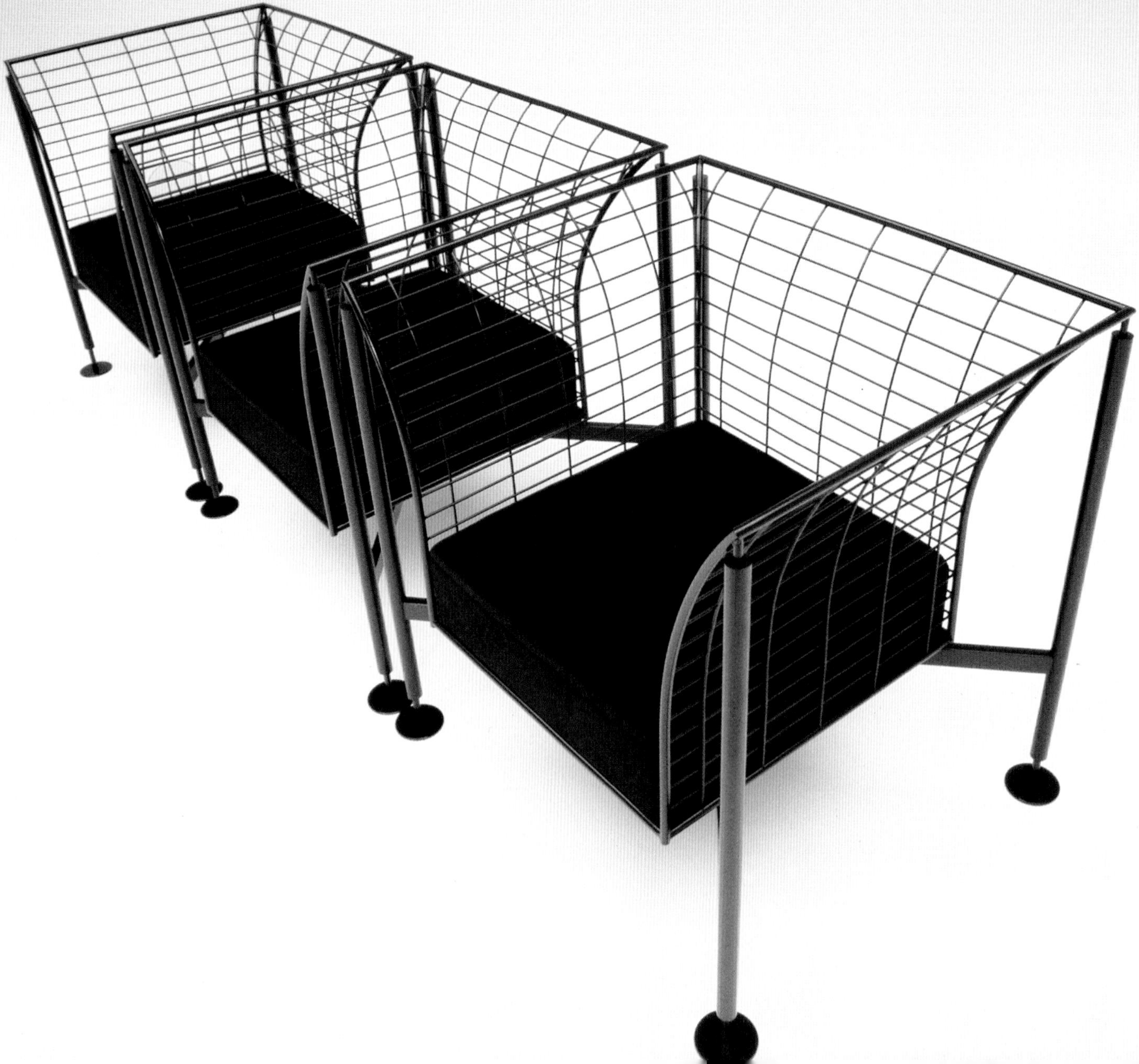

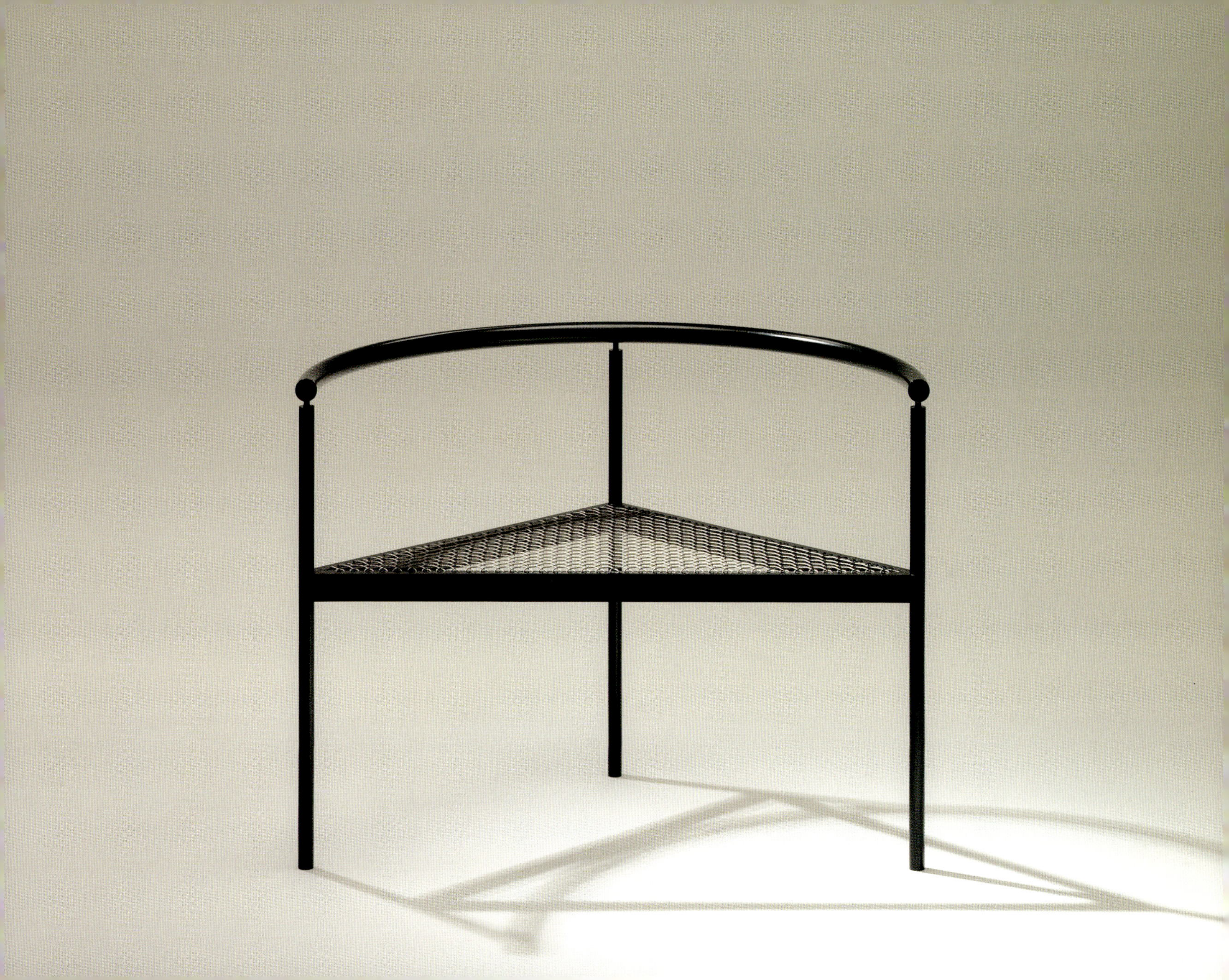

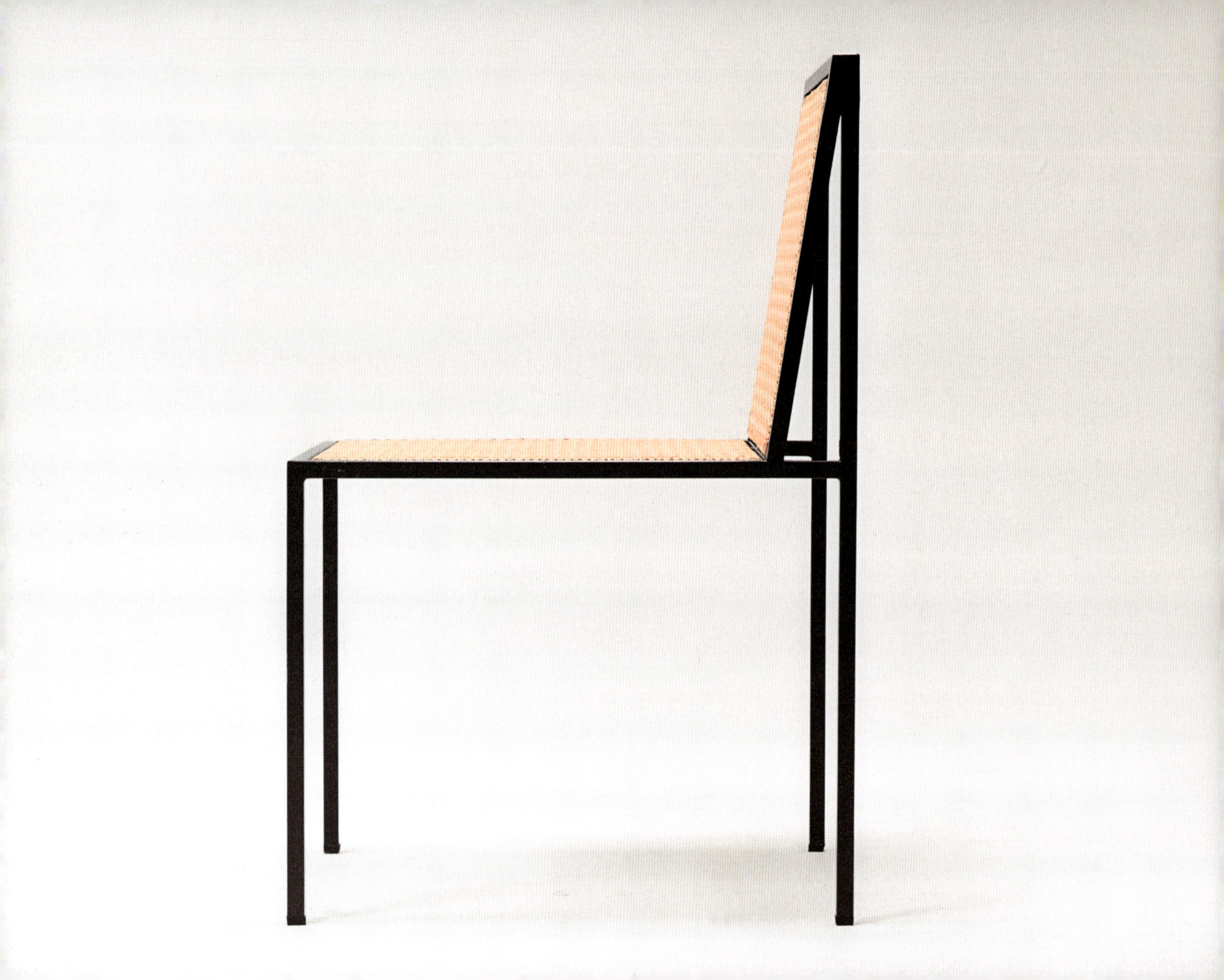

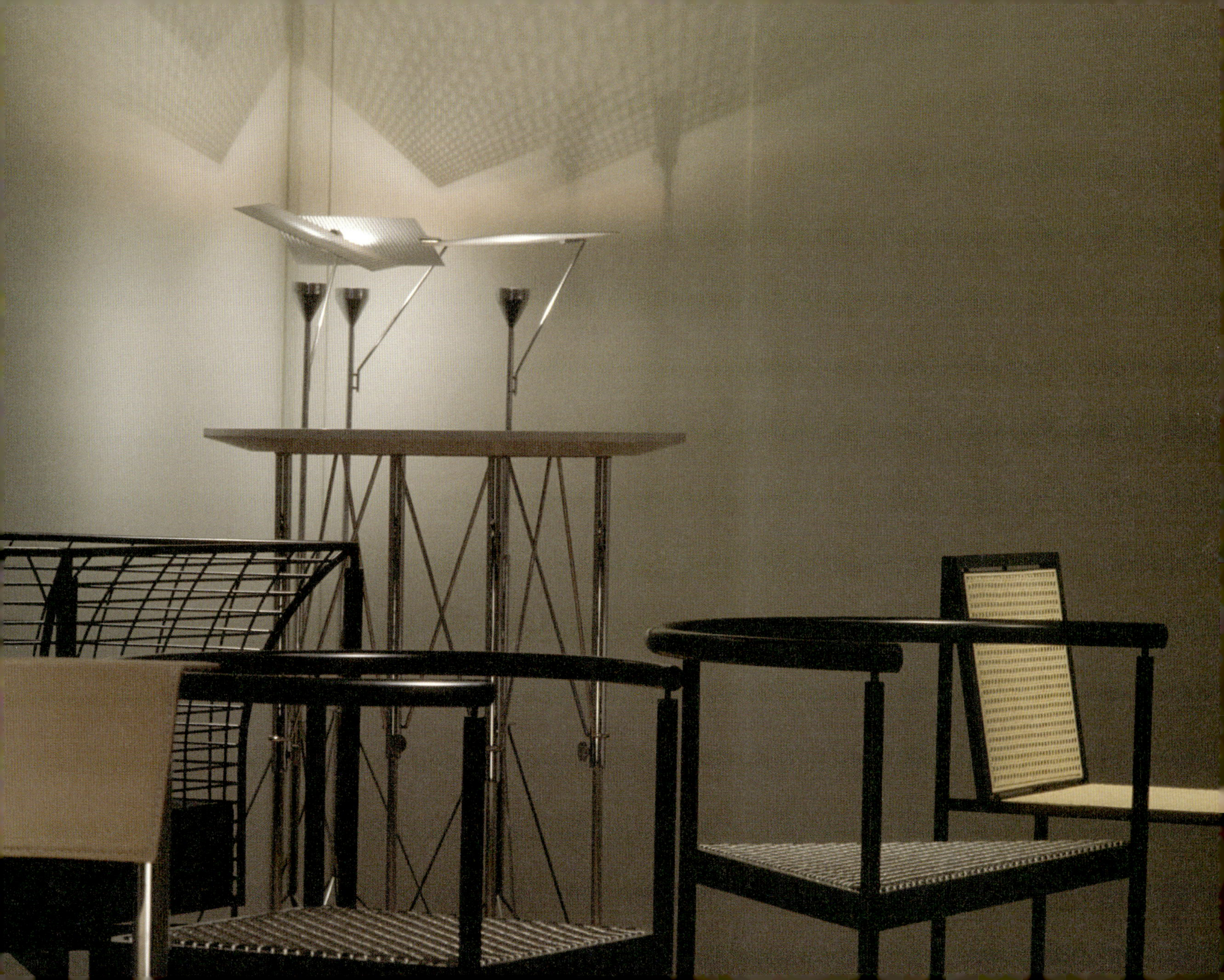

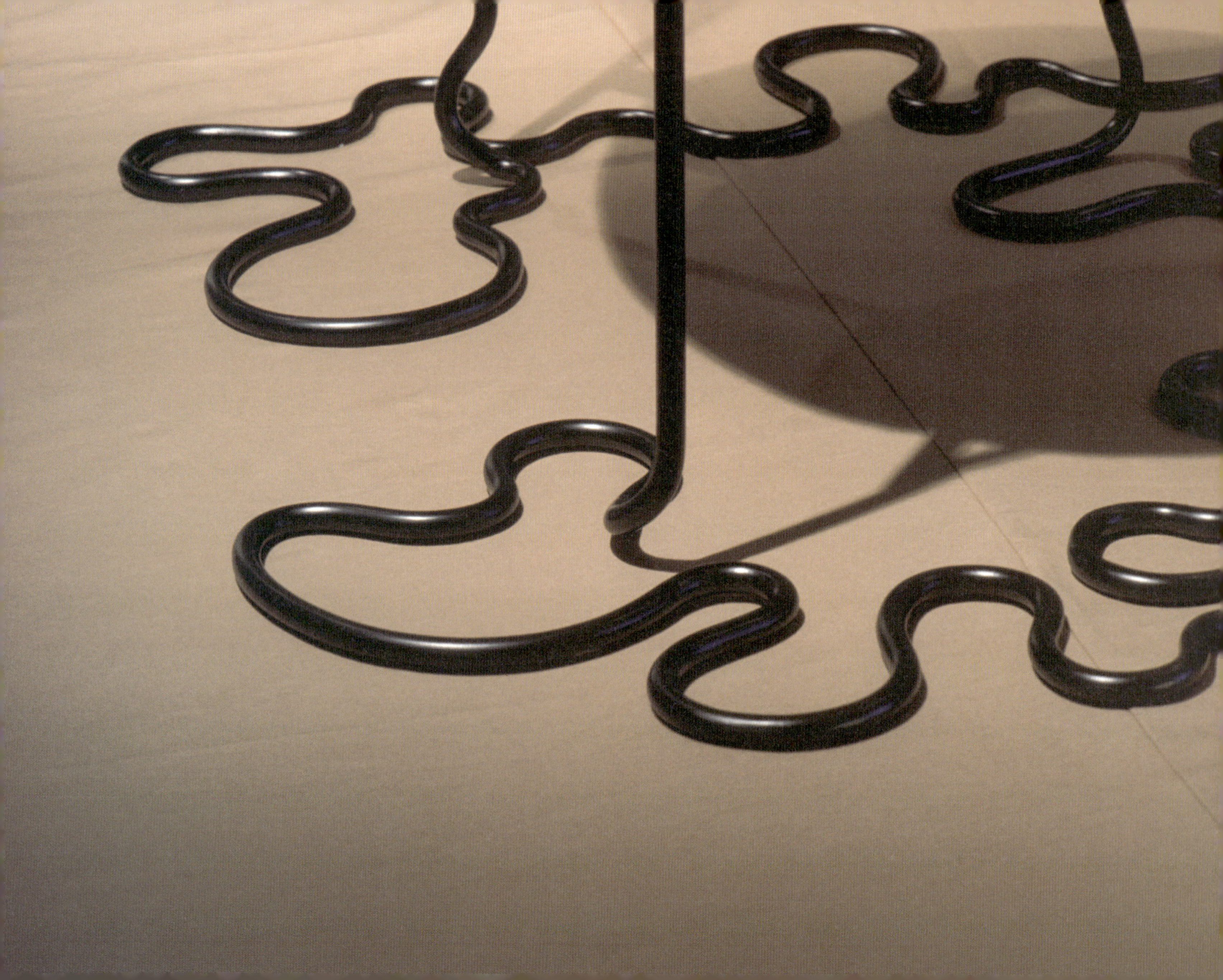

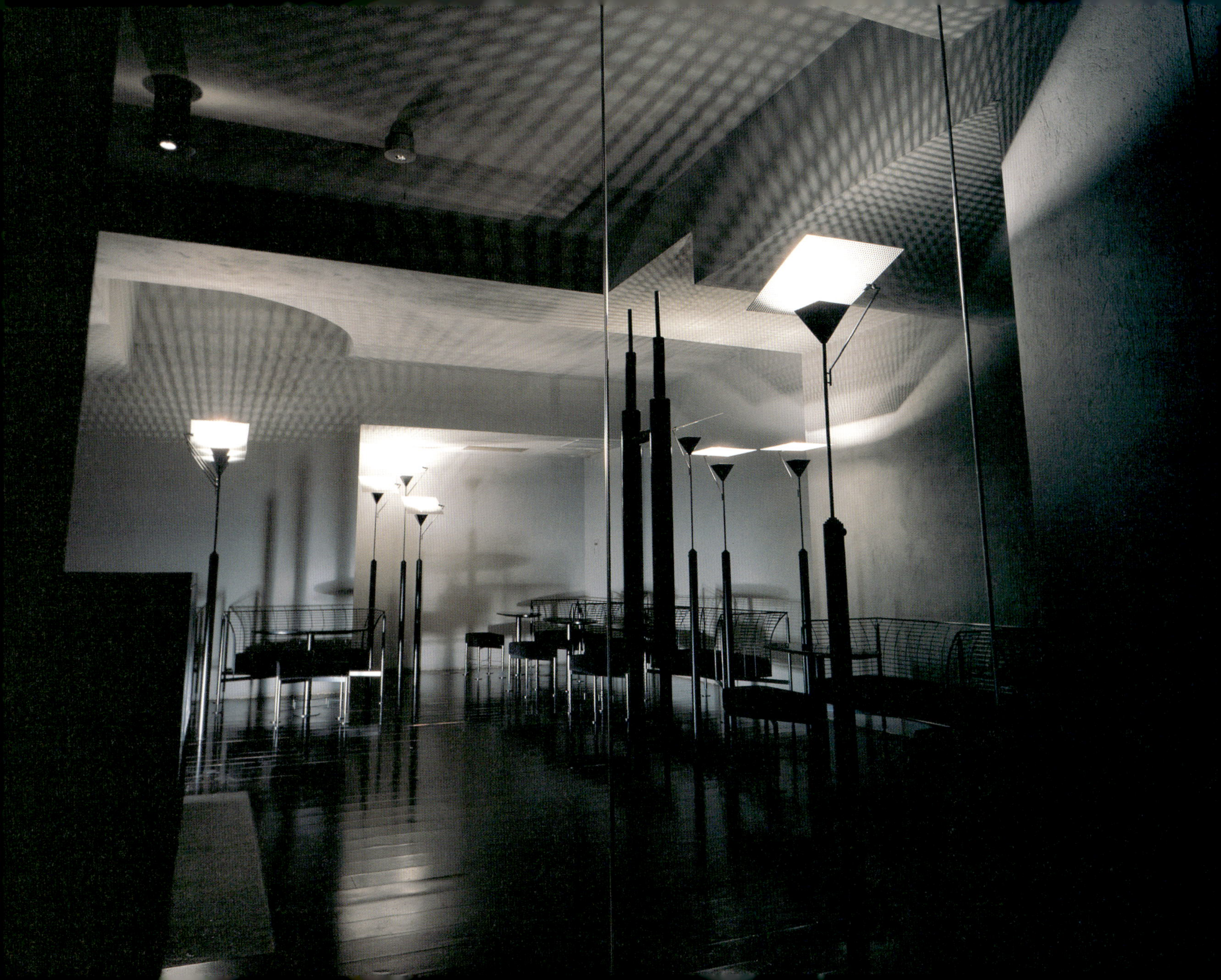

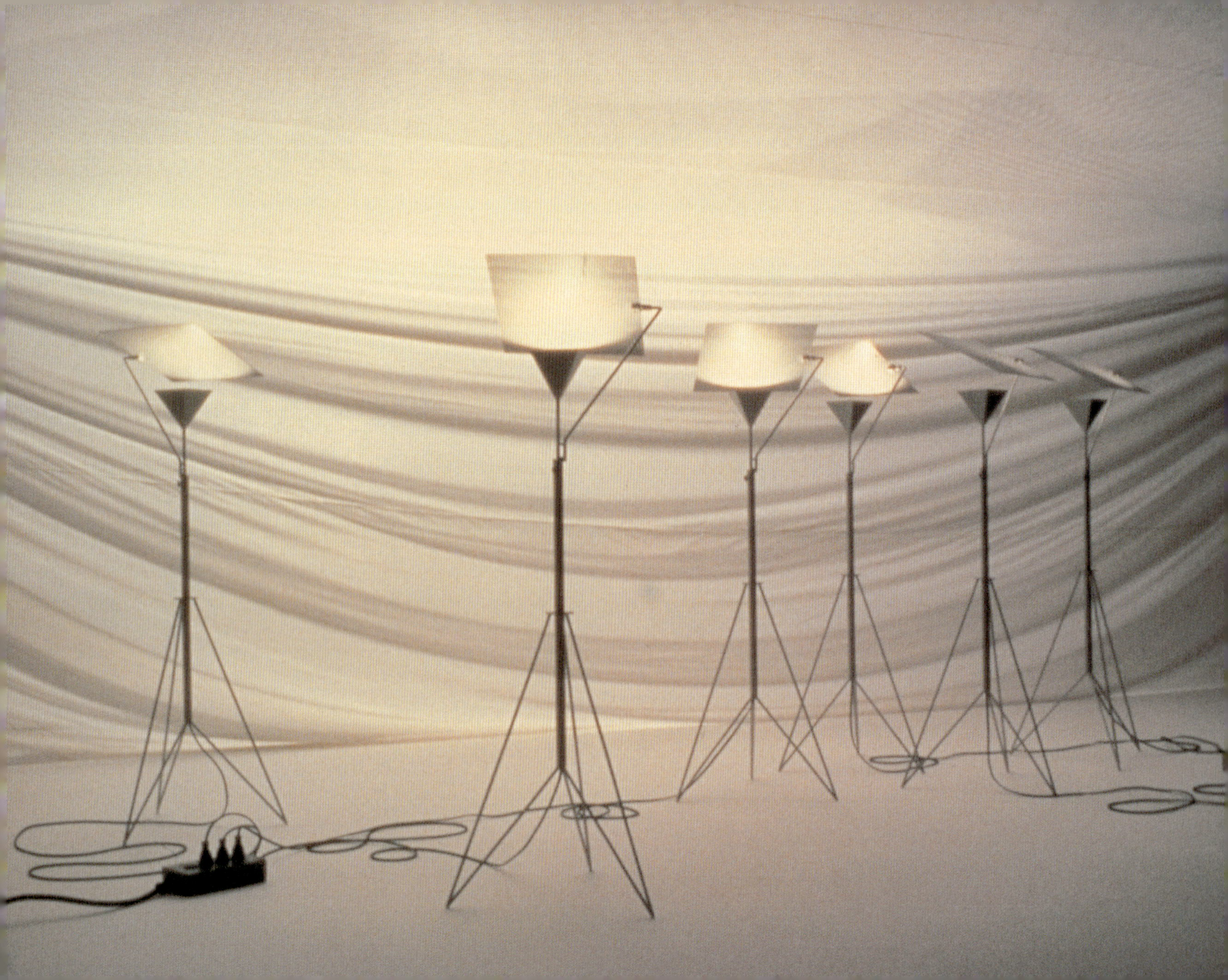

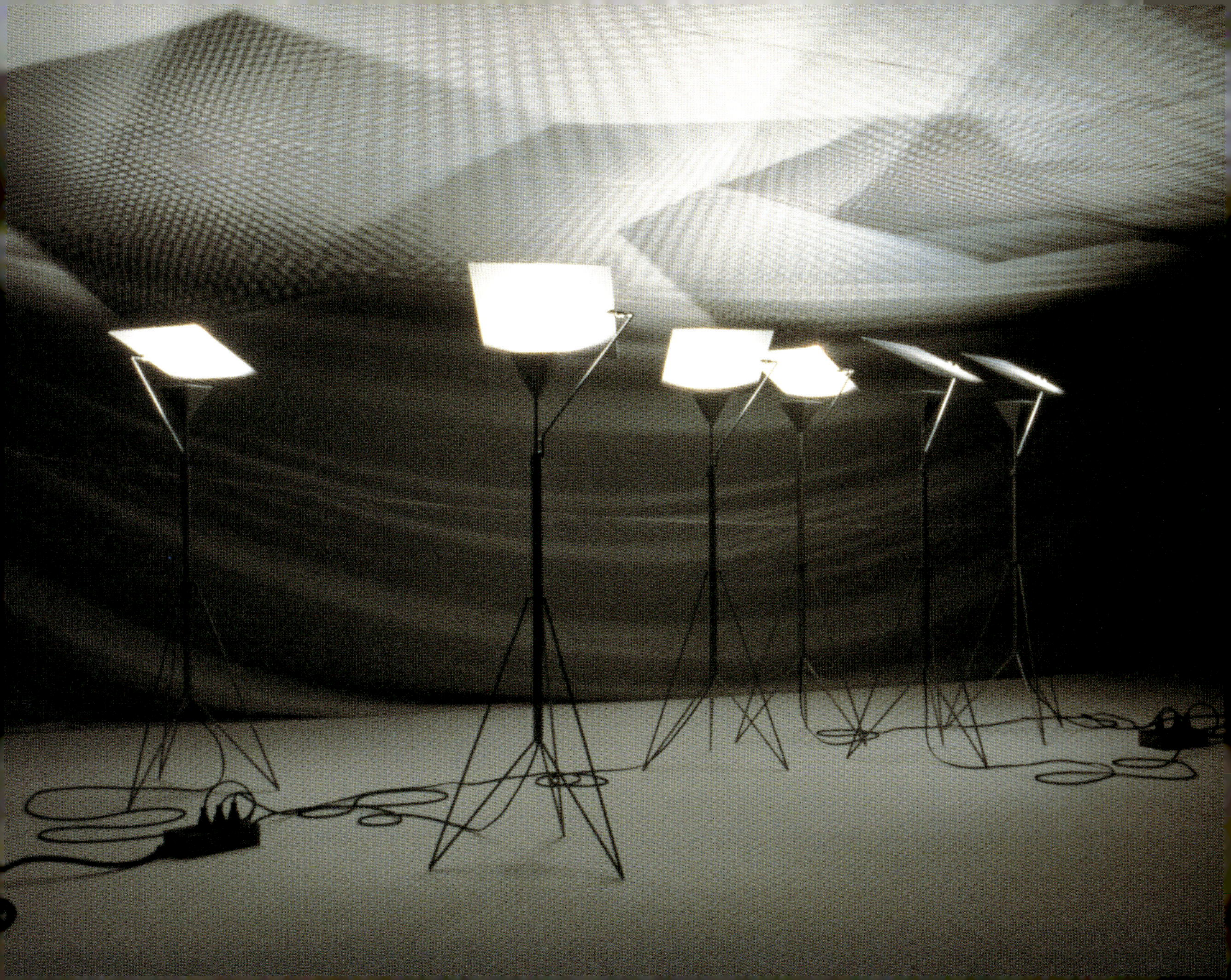

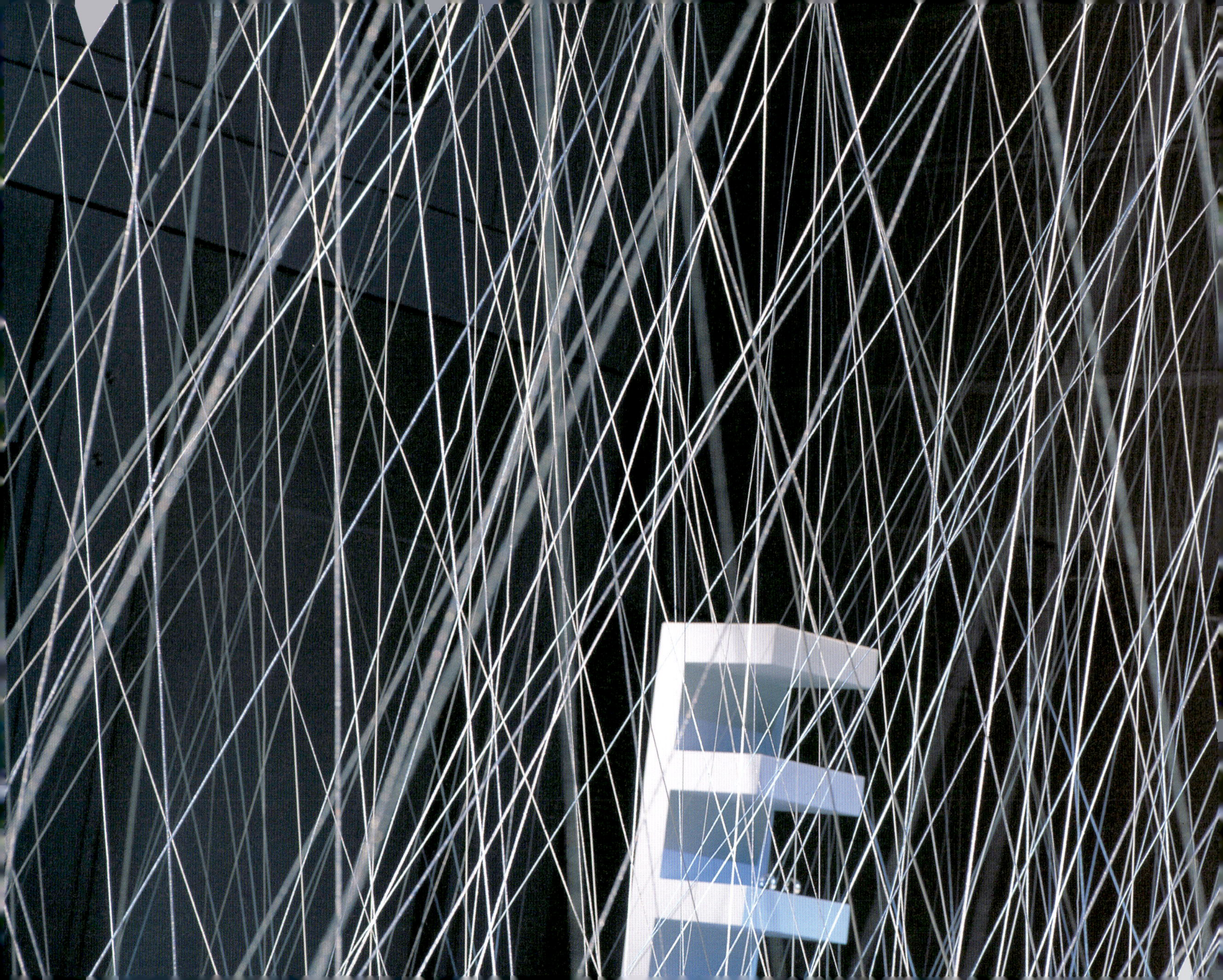

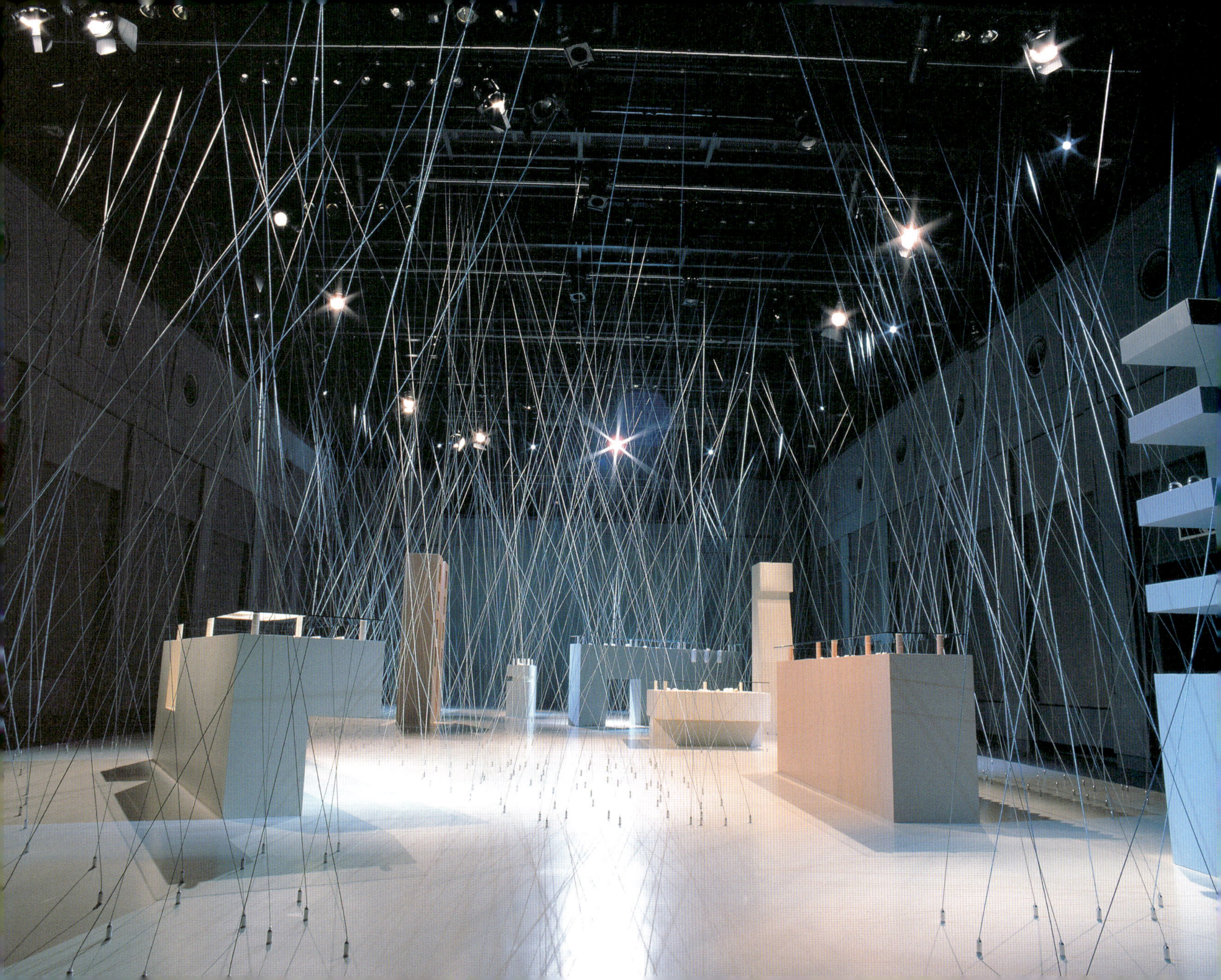

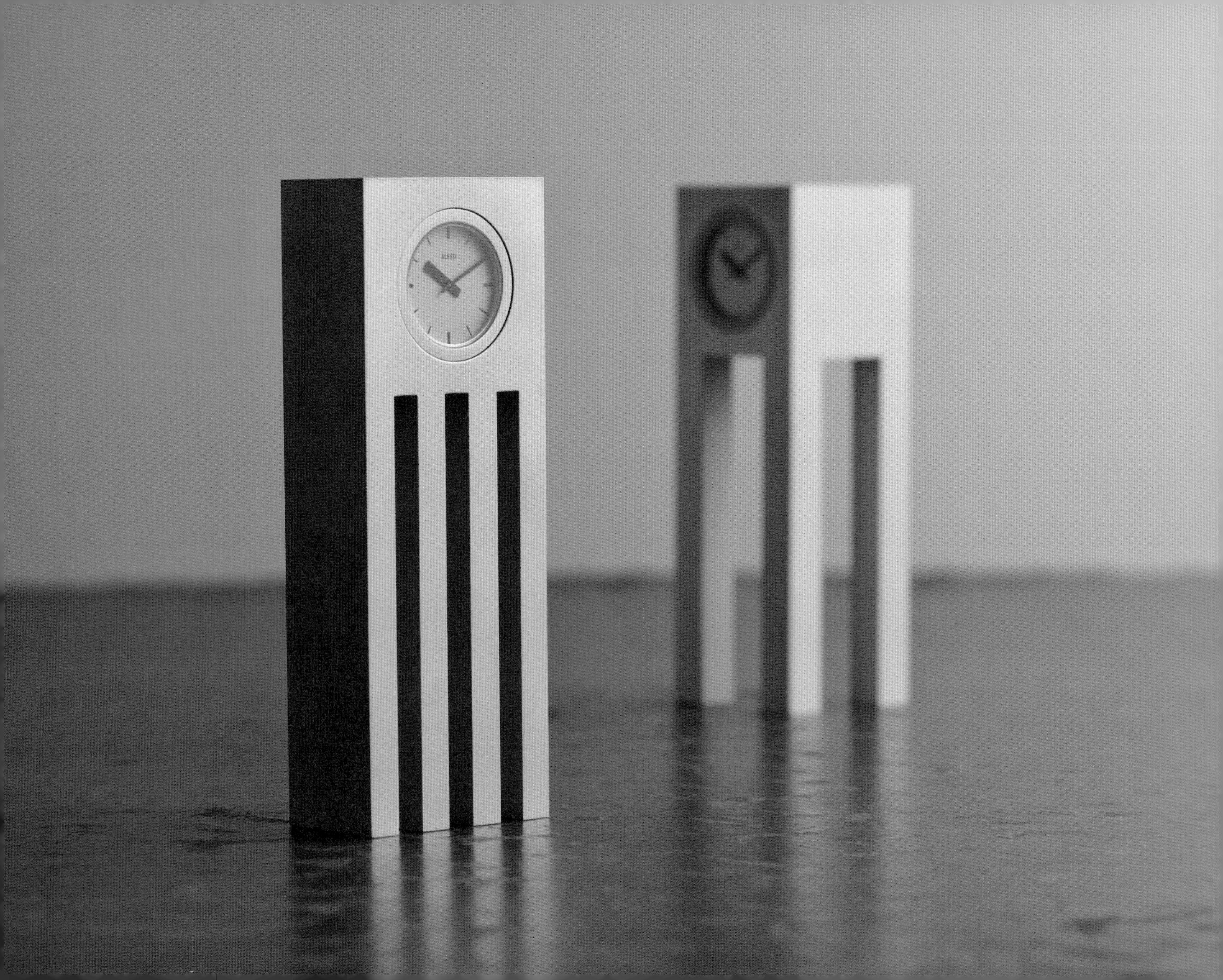

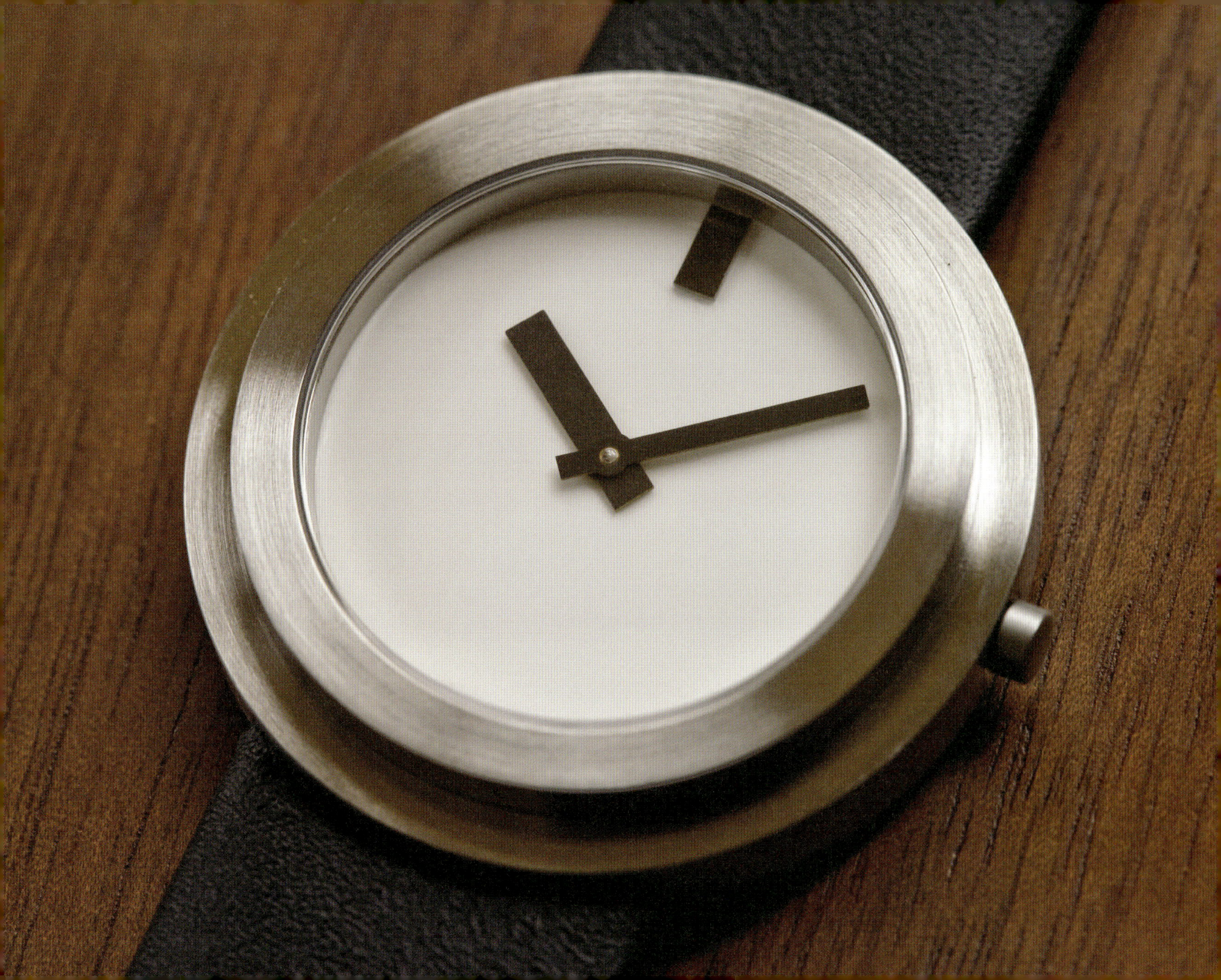

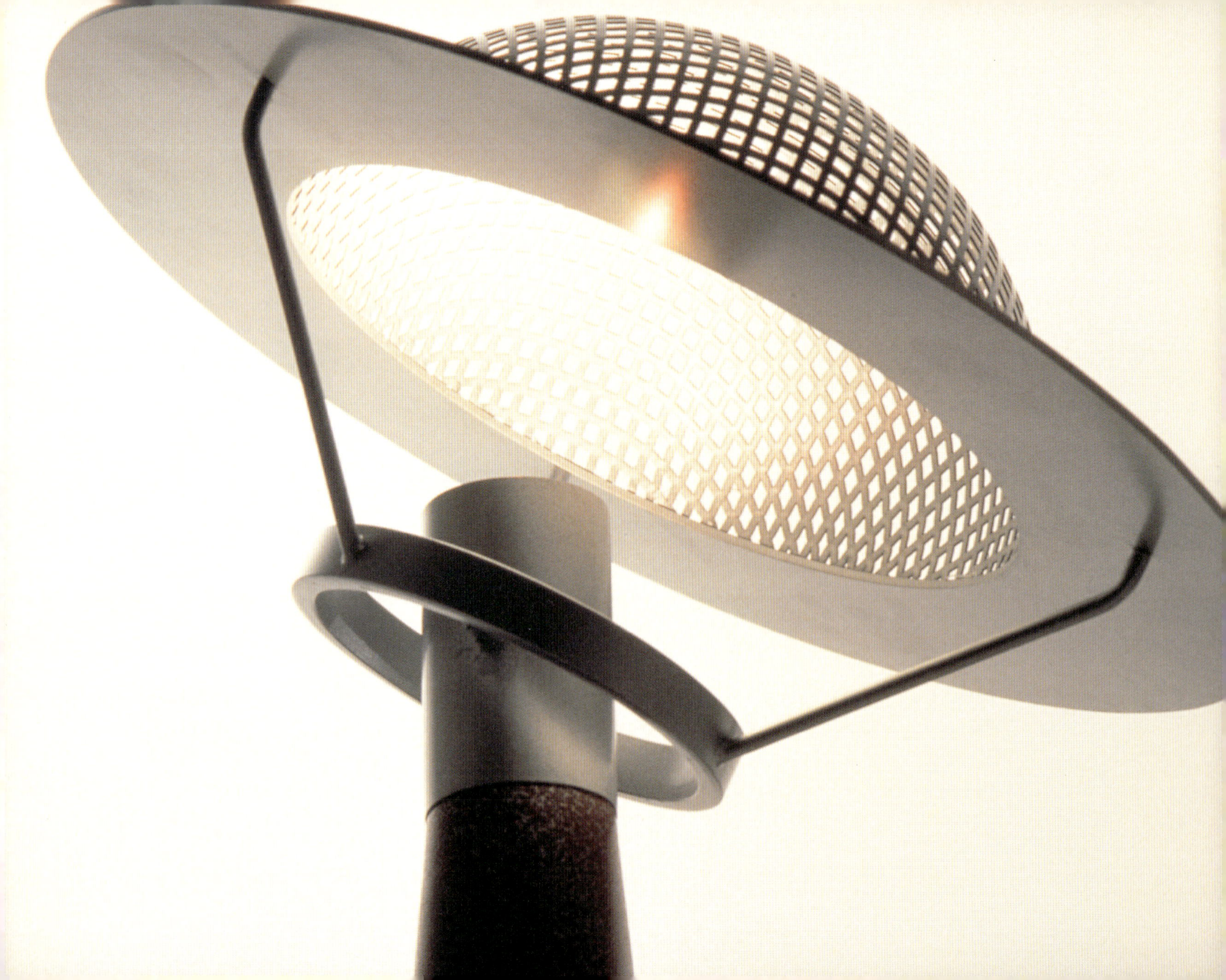

03

しかしそれらの軸や花もそれ自体が装飾の役をしているよりも、
陰翳に深みを添える方が主になっている。
谷崎潤一郎

Rather than serving as decorations in themselves,
the main purpose of those stems and flowers is to add depth to the shadows.
Junichiro Tanizaki

「沓脱ぎ」の行為は聖なる場所へ向かうという意識を
ともなっていると見ることができます。
つまり日本では、家自体が聖なる場所だという認識が強いのではないでしょうか。
内田 繁

In the act of taking off one's shoes before entering the house,
one can see an awareness of entering a sacred place.
That is to say, there is still a strong perception in Japan that the home is a sacred place.
Shigeru Uchida

不自由なるも不自由なりと思う念を生ぜず、
不足なるも不足の念を起さず、
不調なるも不調の念を抱かぬを侘びなりと心得べきなり。
千宗旦

To not feel discomfort even when discomforted,
to not feel poverty even when poor,
to not mind when things go wrong, now that is *wabi*.
Sen no Sotan

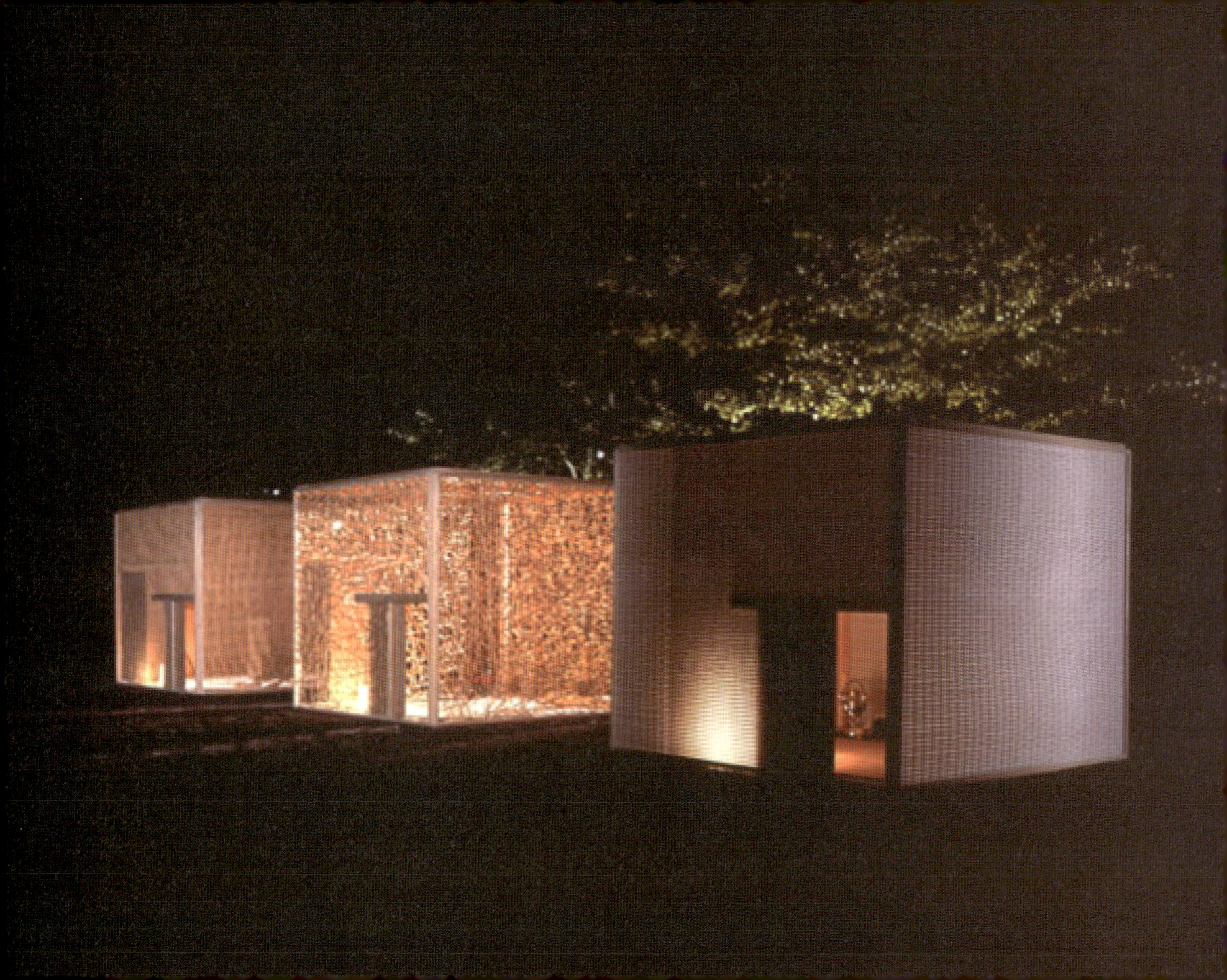

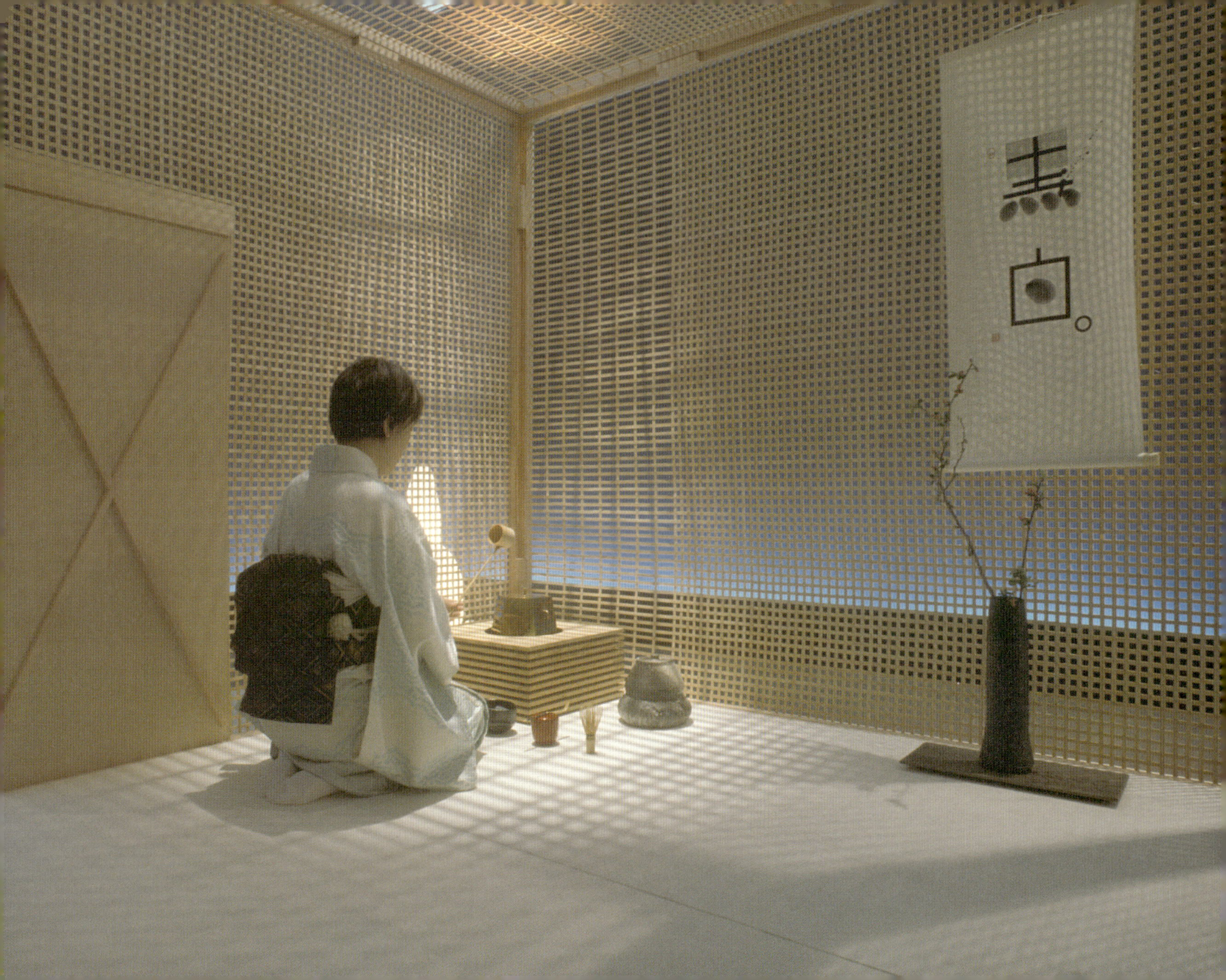

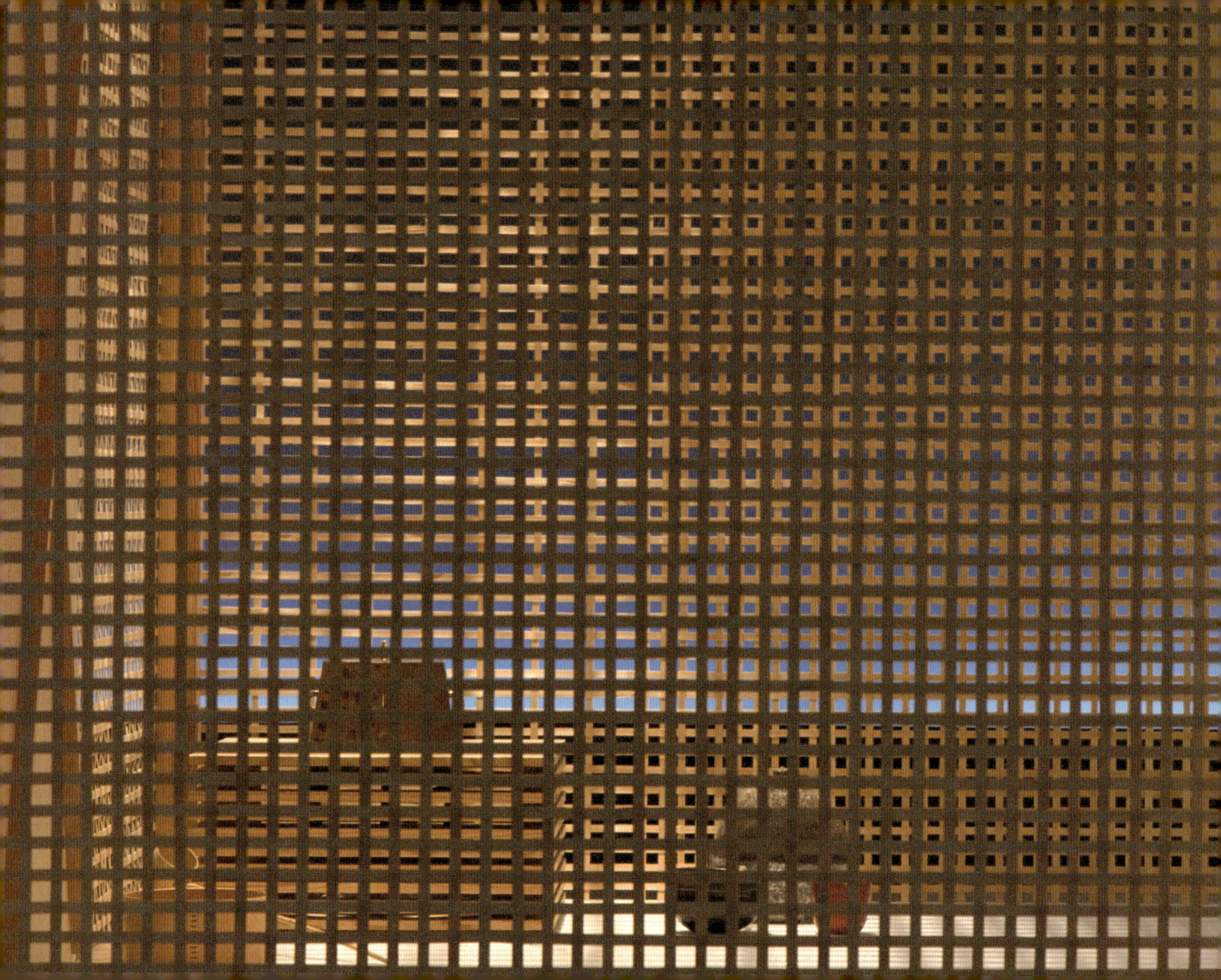

黑白。

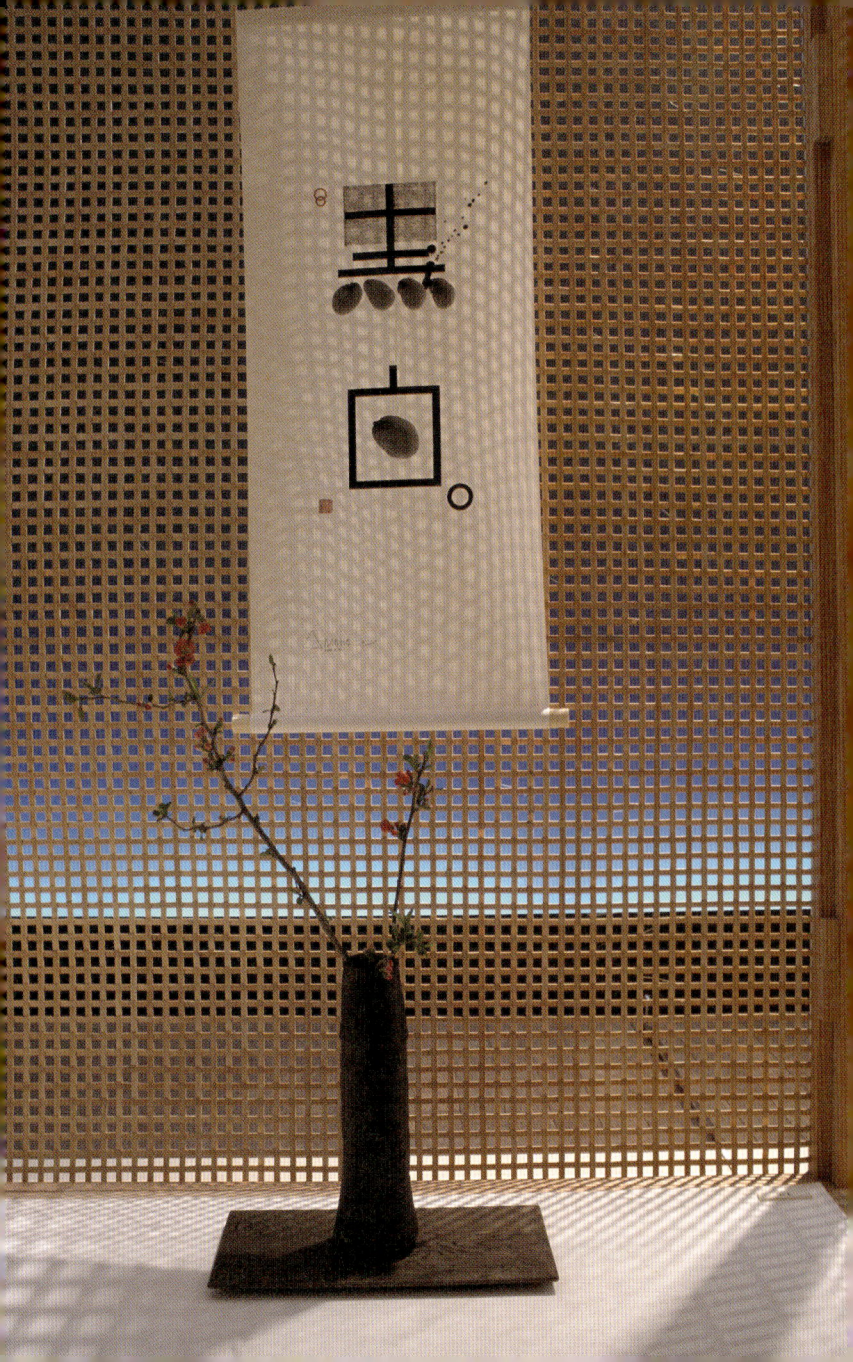

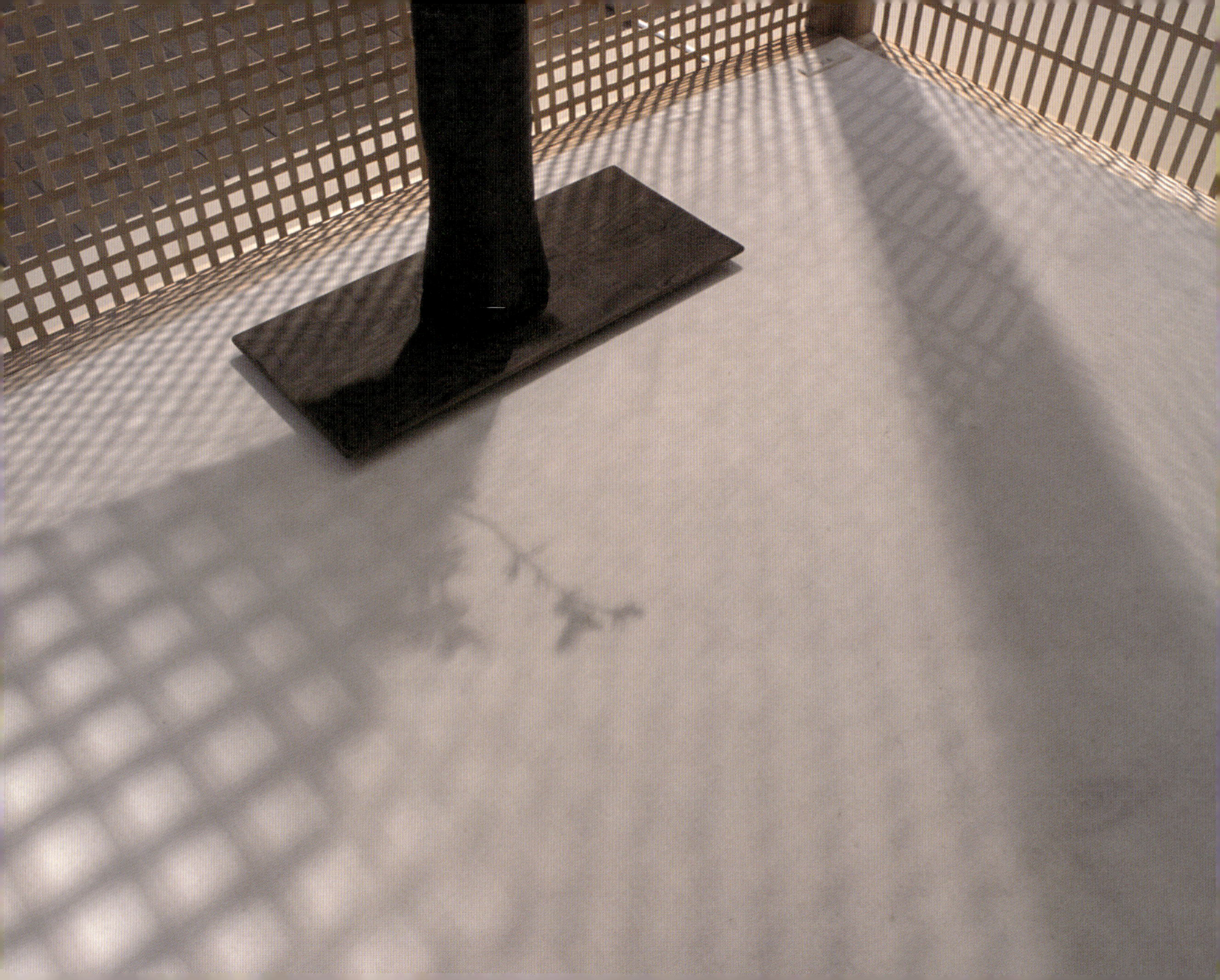

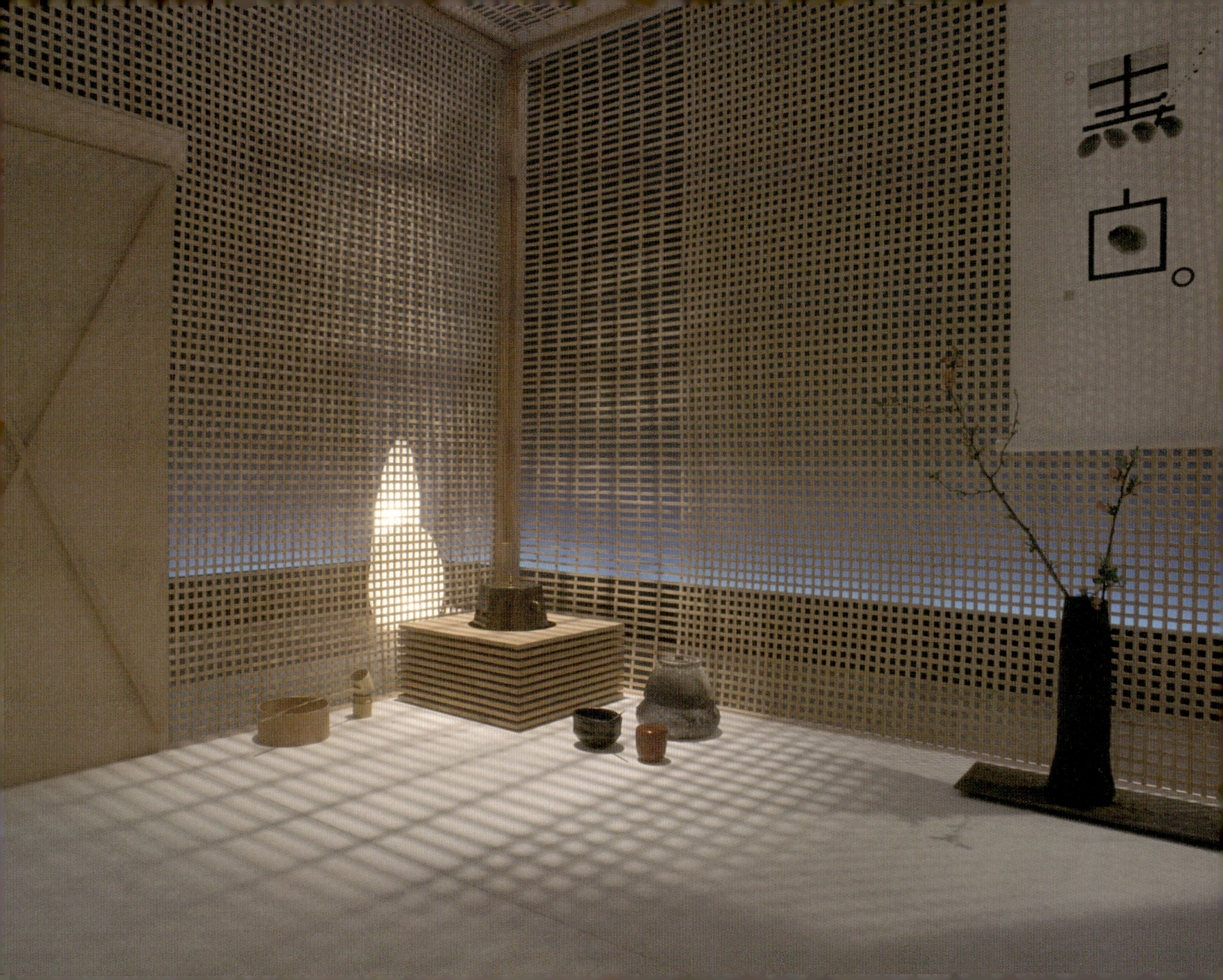

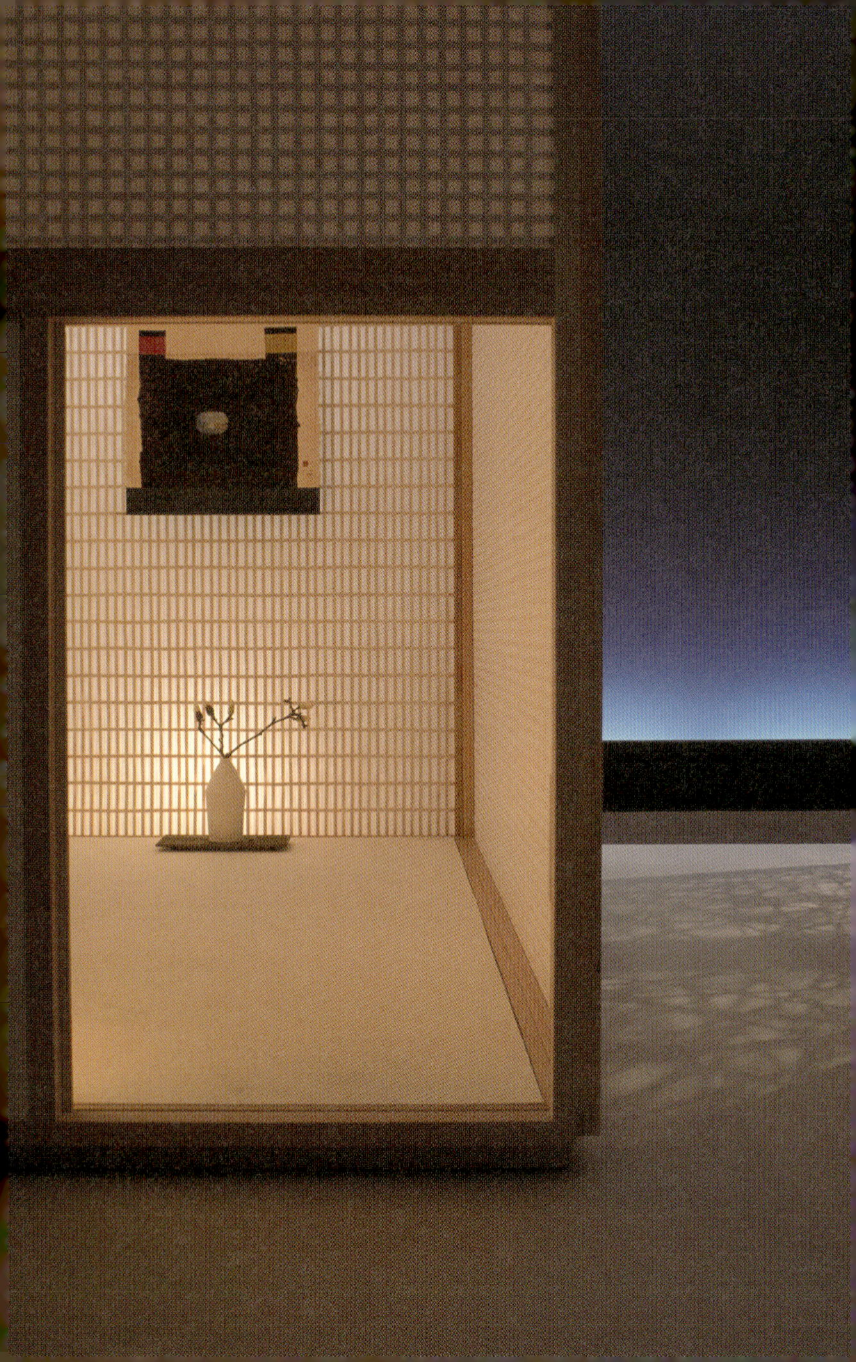

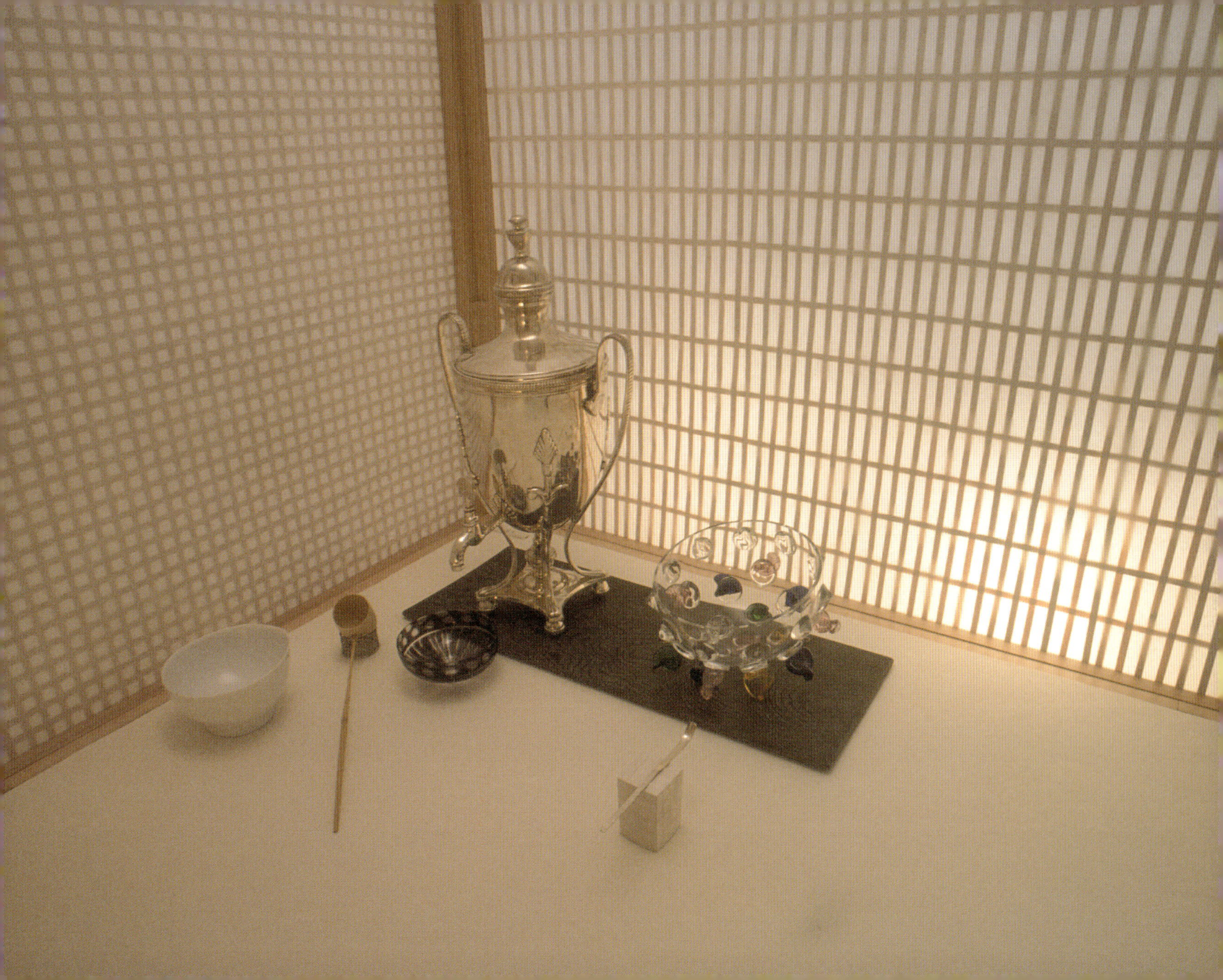

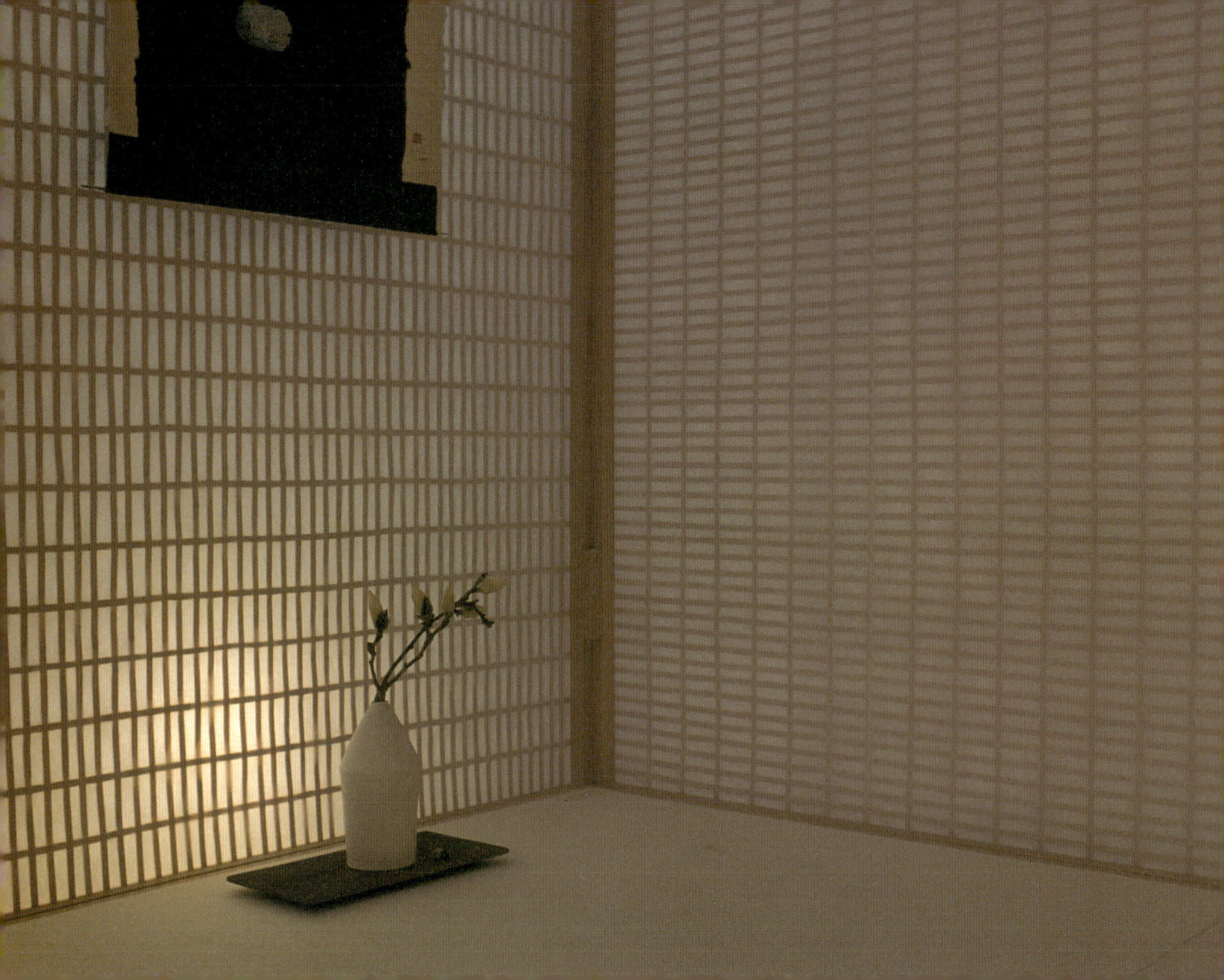

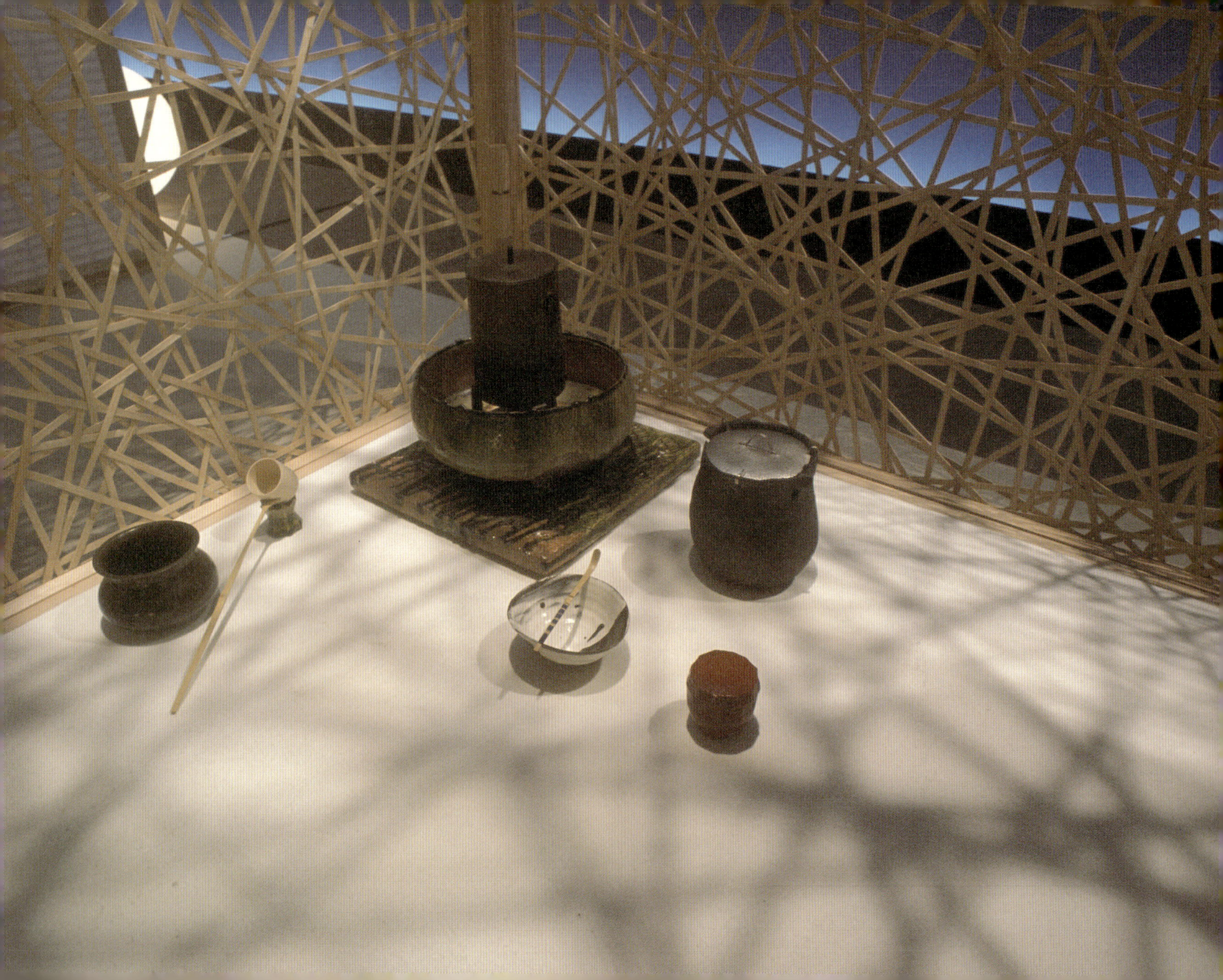

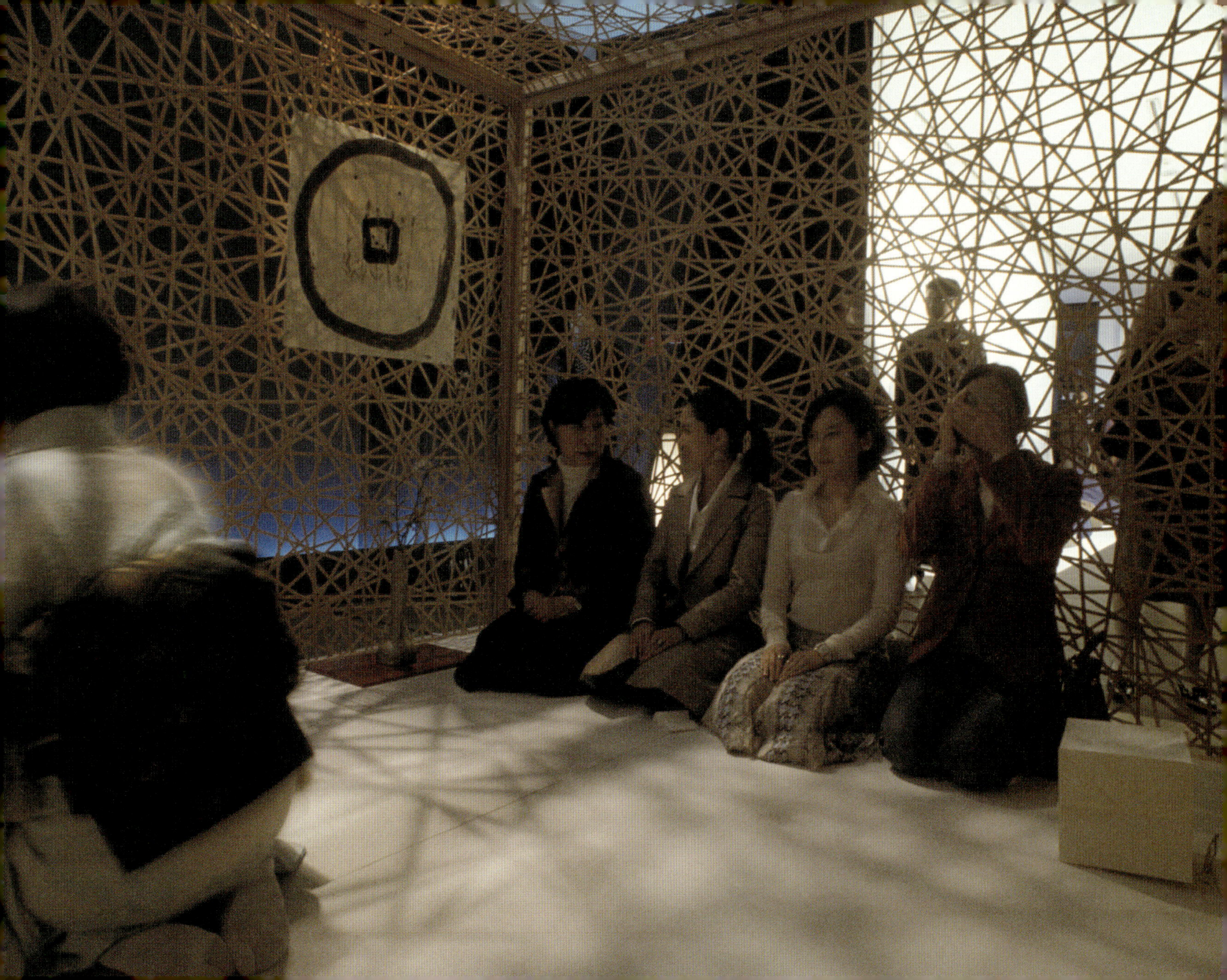

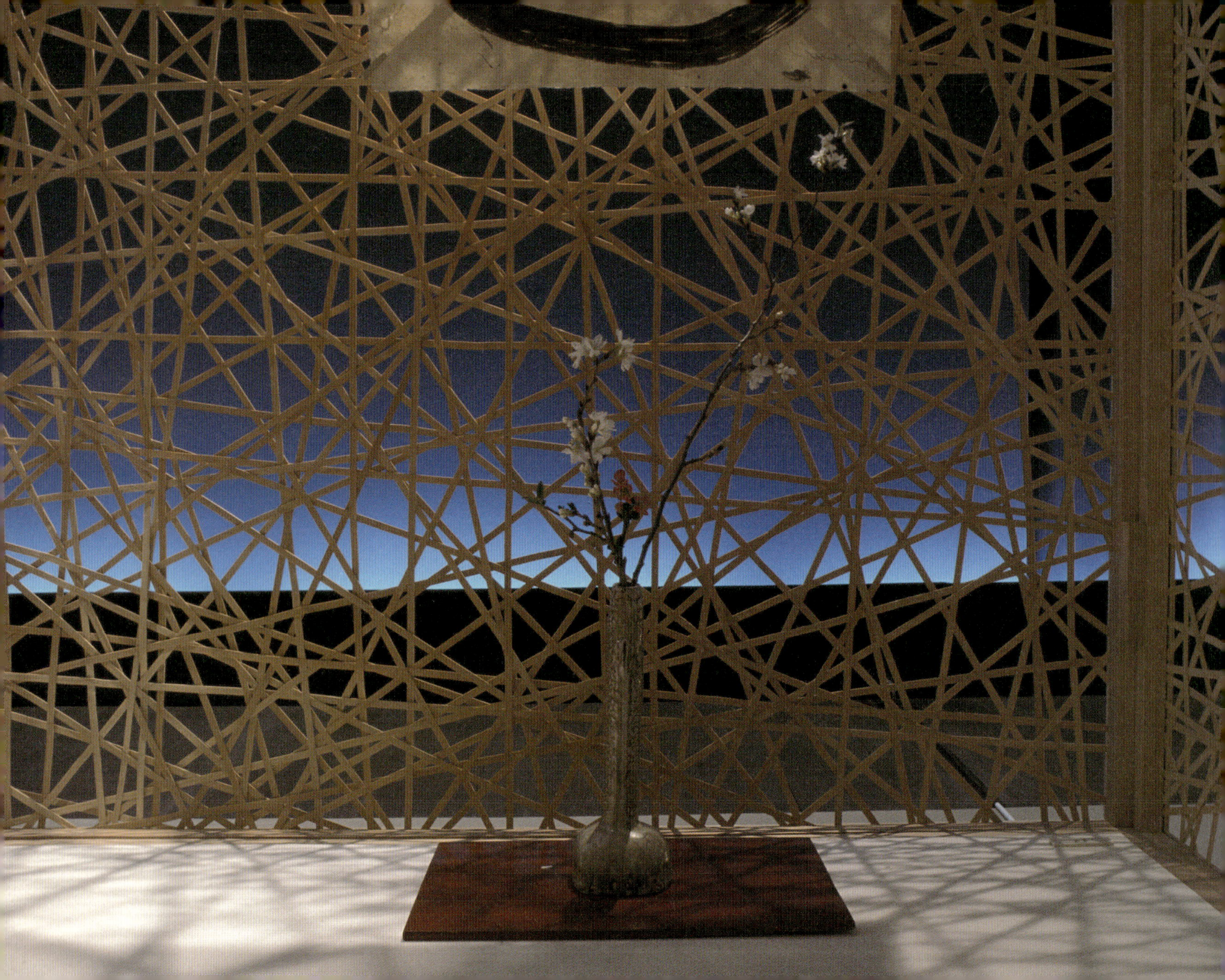

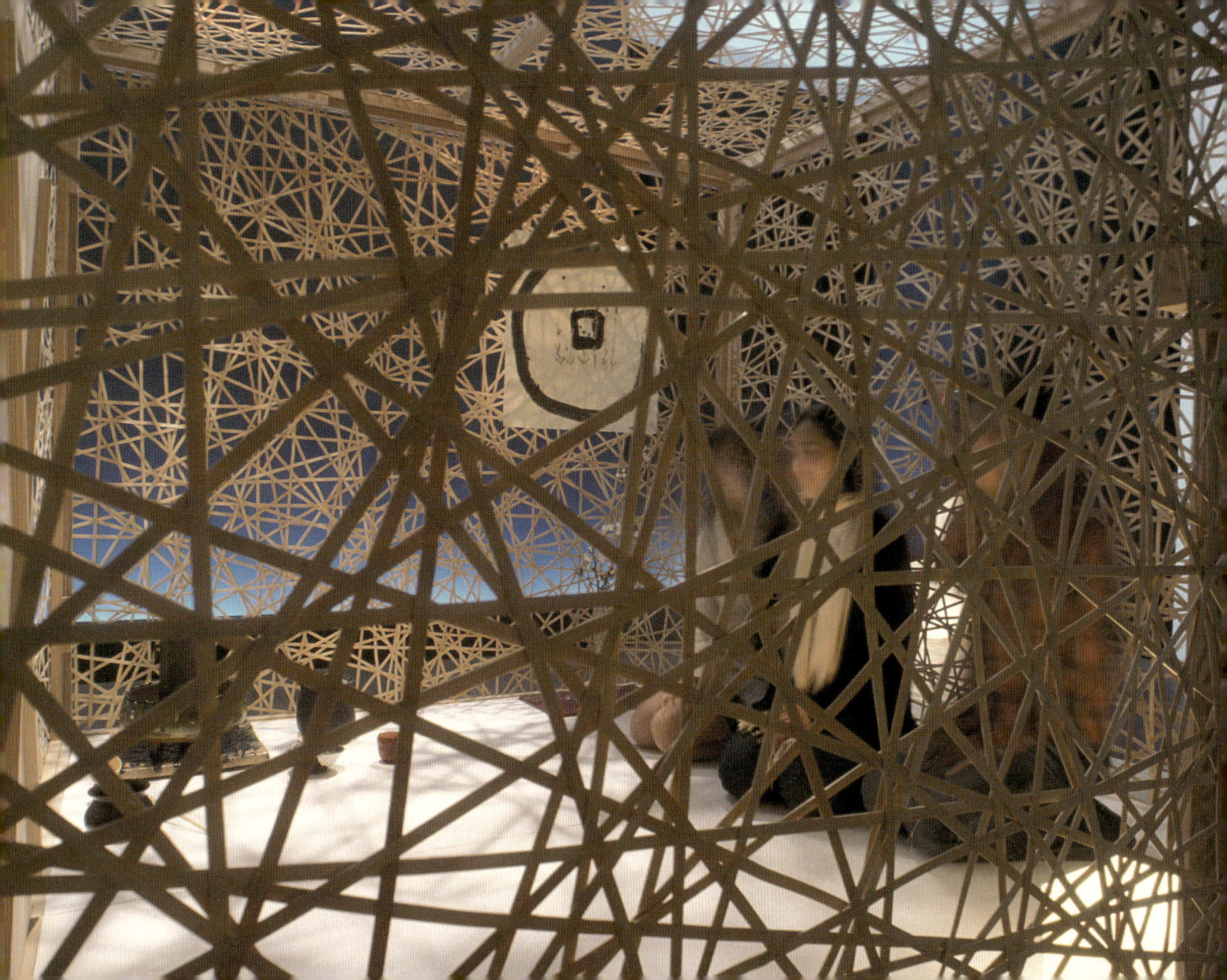

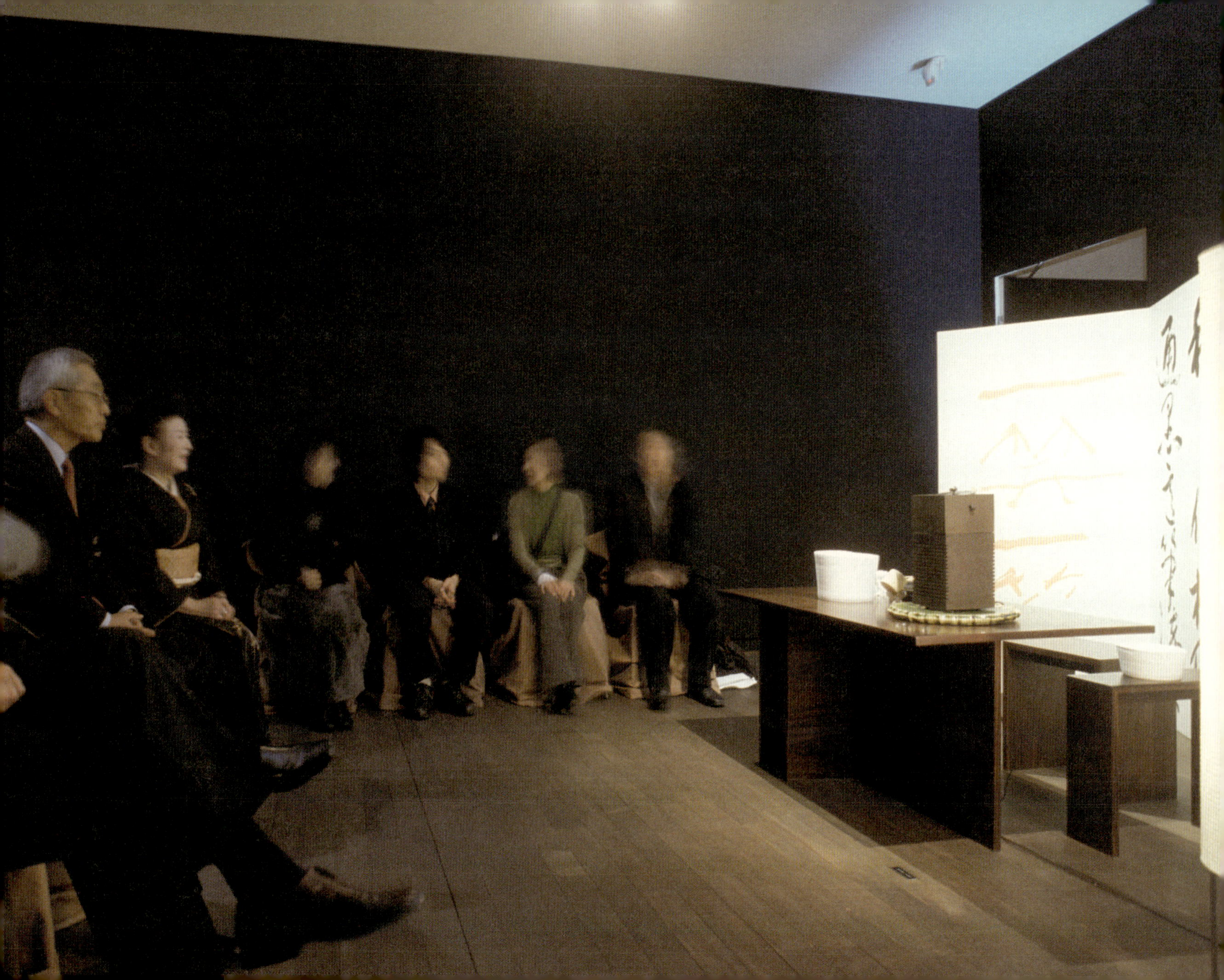

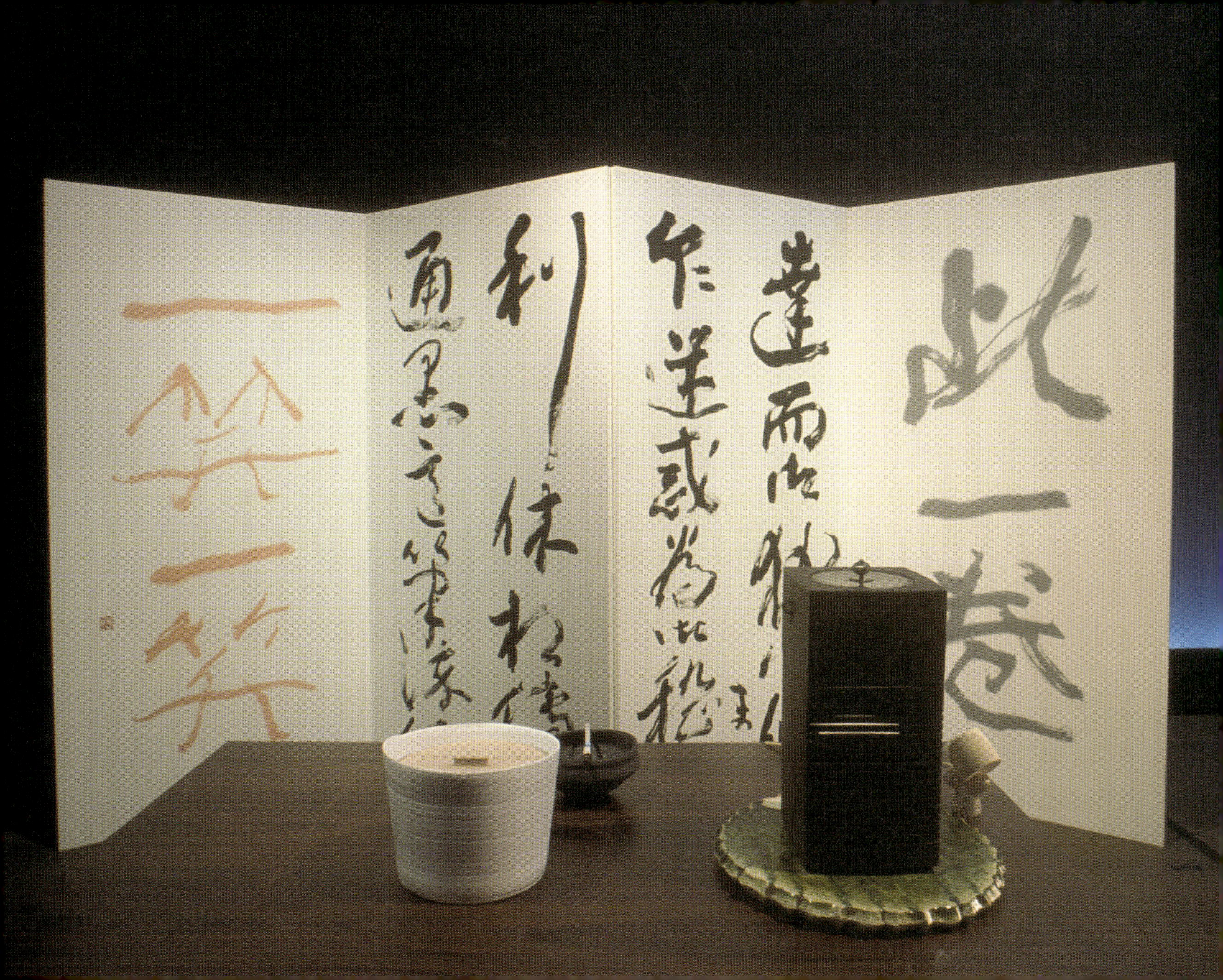

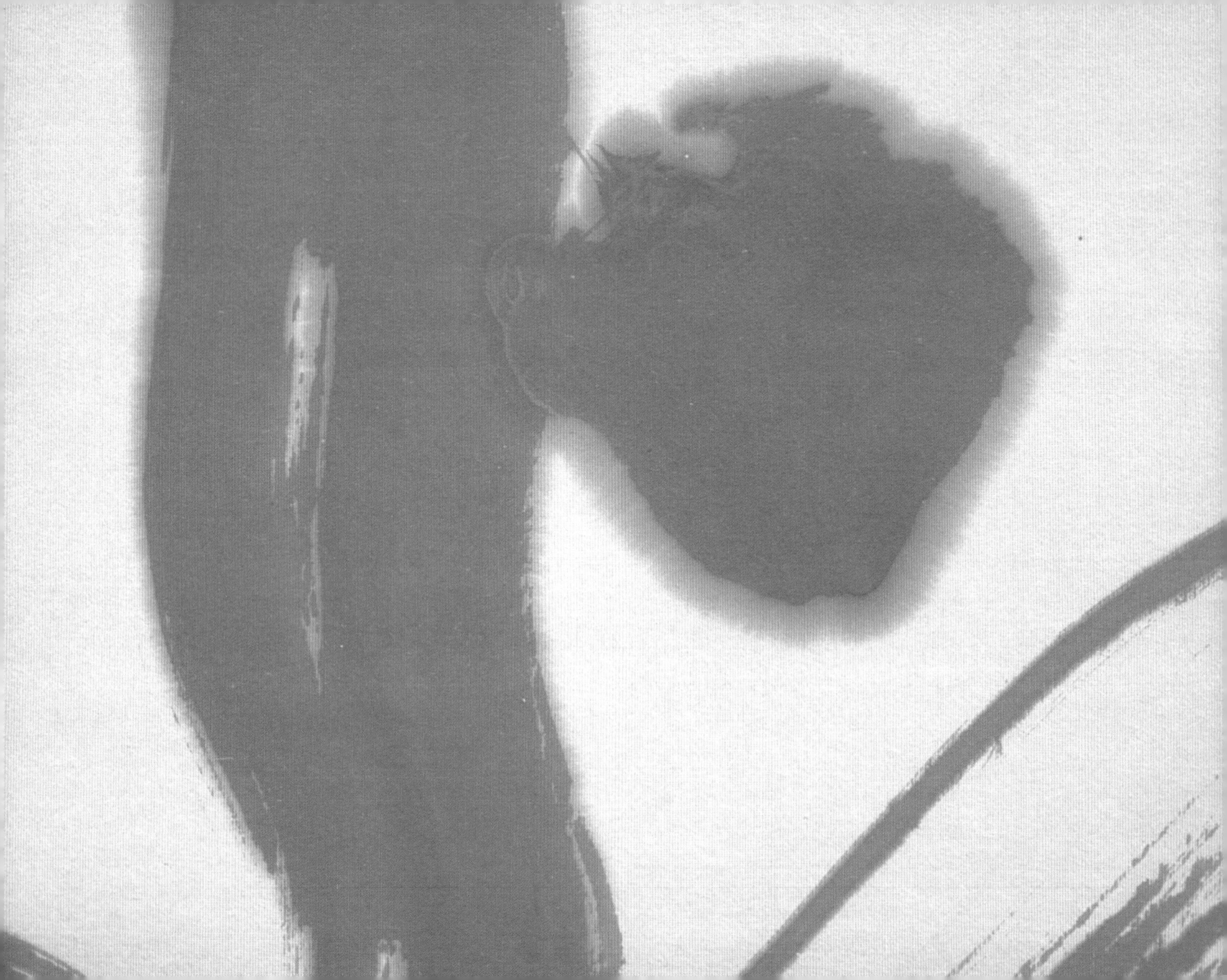

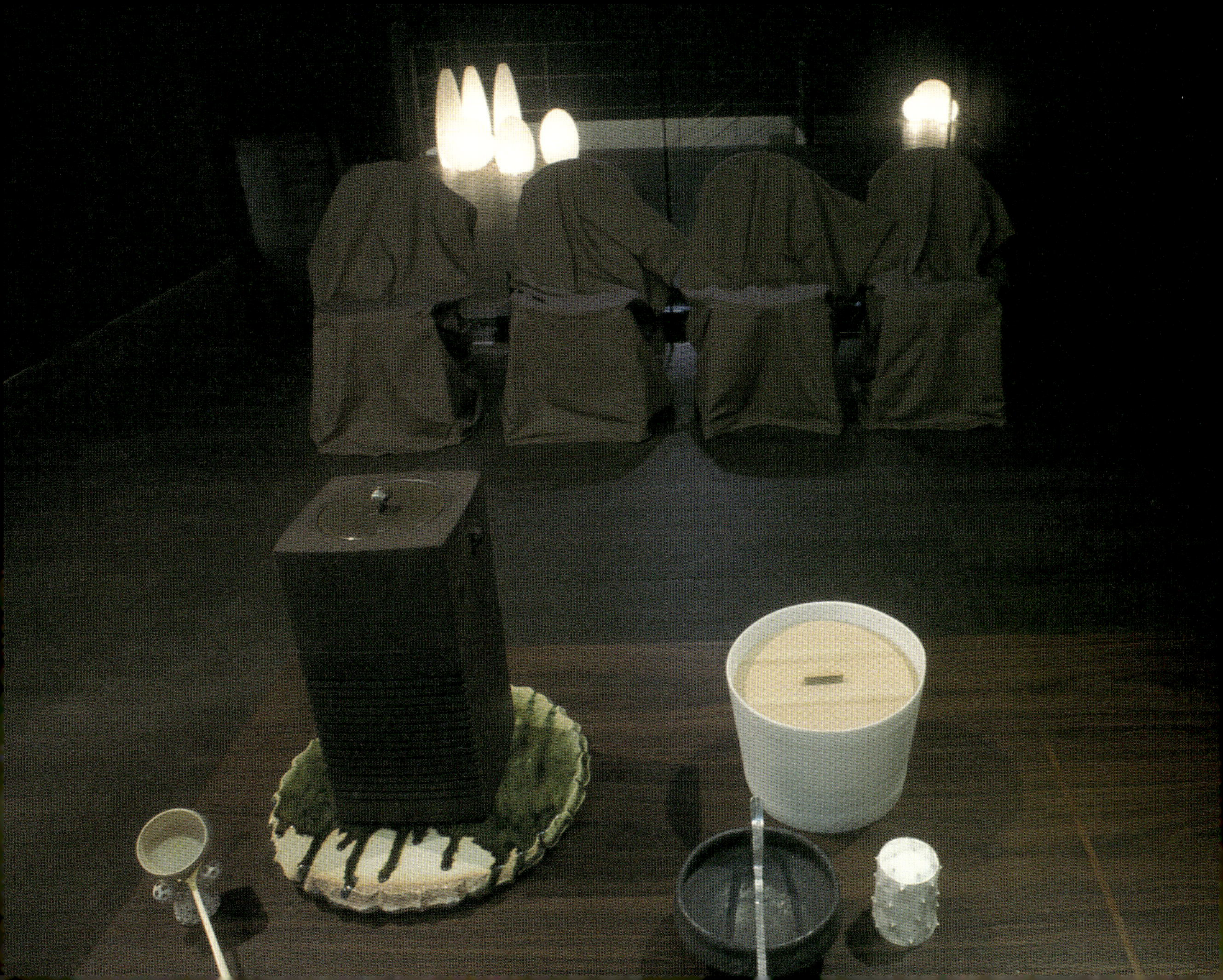

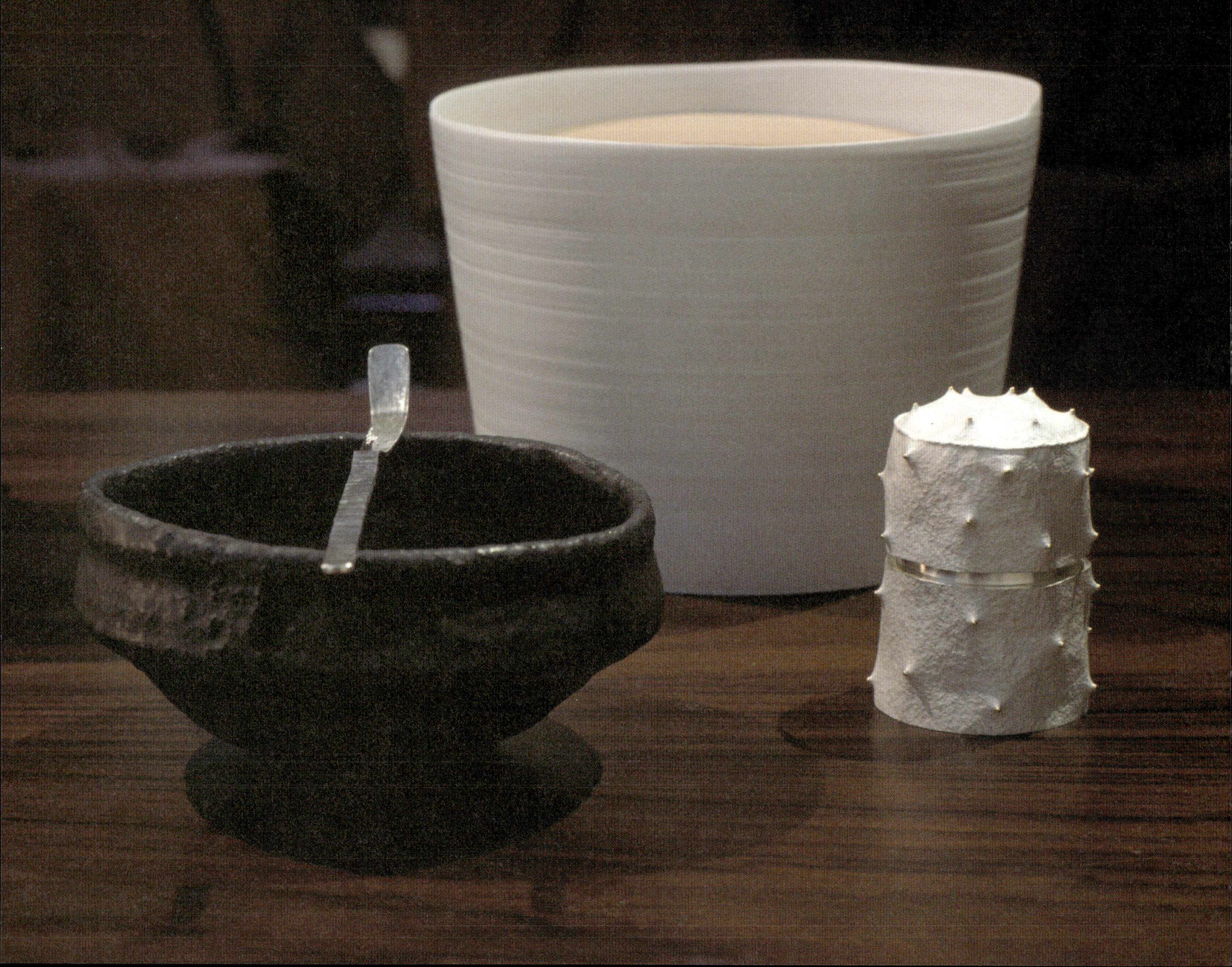

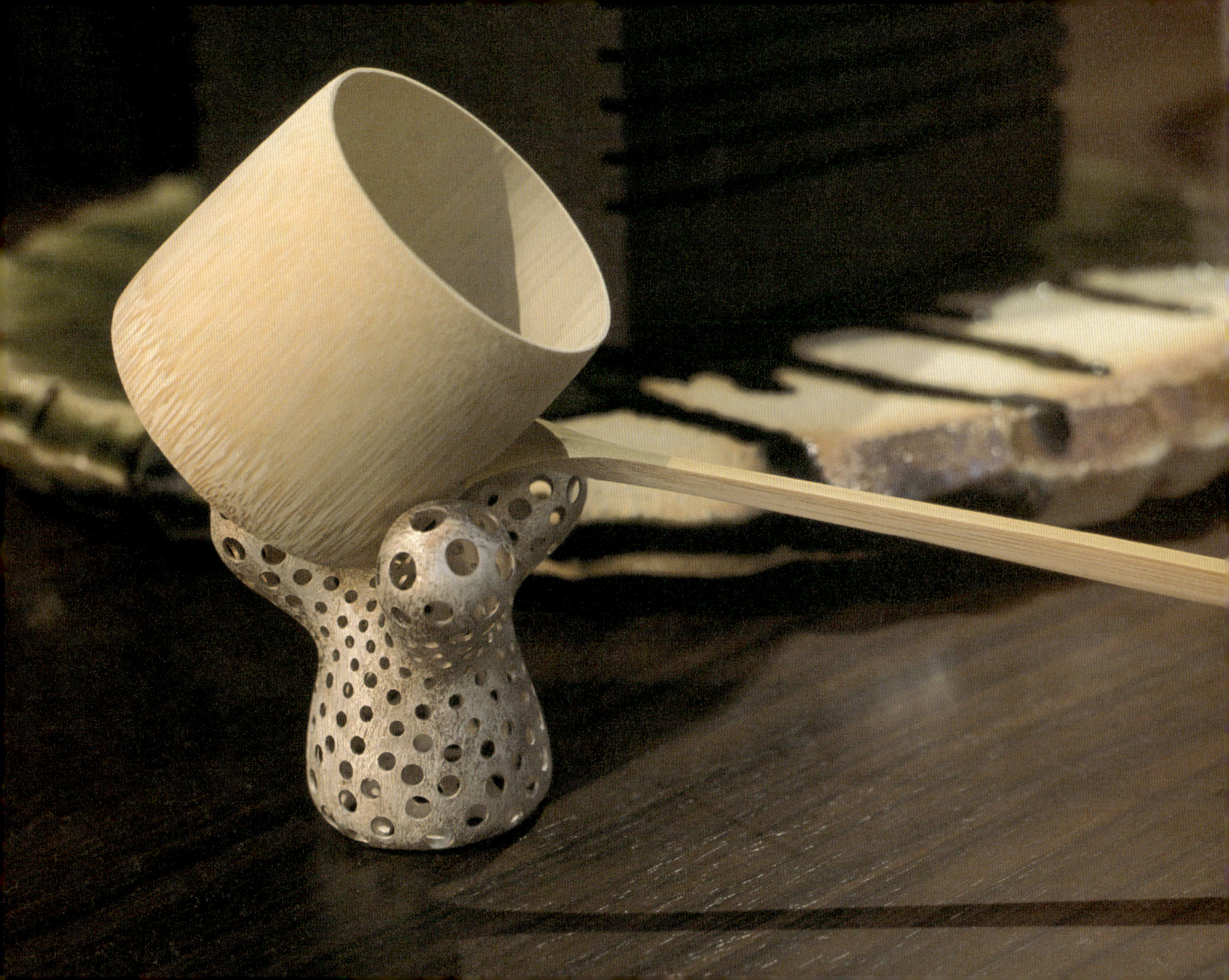

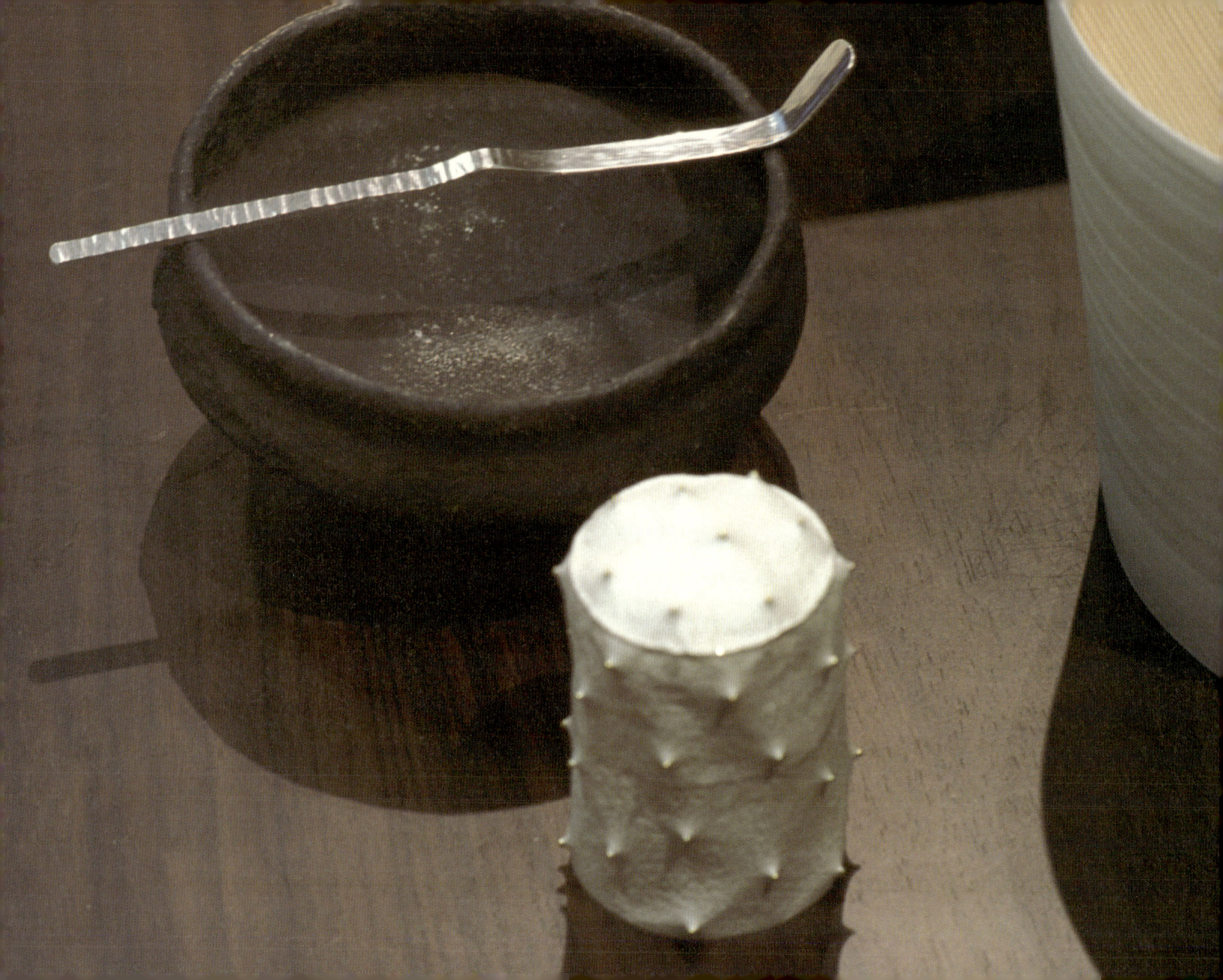

04

外見上、別に間違った点がないからと云って、
なにがそれで充分なものか！
稲垣足穂

There may not seem to be anything particularly wrong on the surface,
but how could you think even for a moment that that is sufficient.
Taruho Inagaki

近代は全体をまず考え、部分をそれに当てはめてきました。
今日重要なのは、断片、部分など小さな世界や身近なテーマ、
「小さな物語」から出発することだと思います。
内田 繁

In the age of modernity, you used to start by considering the whole and then adjust
the various parts accordingly. Now, however, I think it is important to start anew
from the fragments and parts, the "little stories" of a smaller world and familiar themes.
Shigeru Uchida

花と、面白きと、珍しきと、これ三つは、同じ心なり。
いづれの花が散らで残るべき。
散る故によりて、咲く比あれば、珍しきなり。
世阿弥元清

Flowers, attractiveness and rarity are all the same:
sooner or later, the petals will fall.
But it precisely because they are destined to fall that they move you when in blossom.
Zeami Motokiyo

StarAlpha

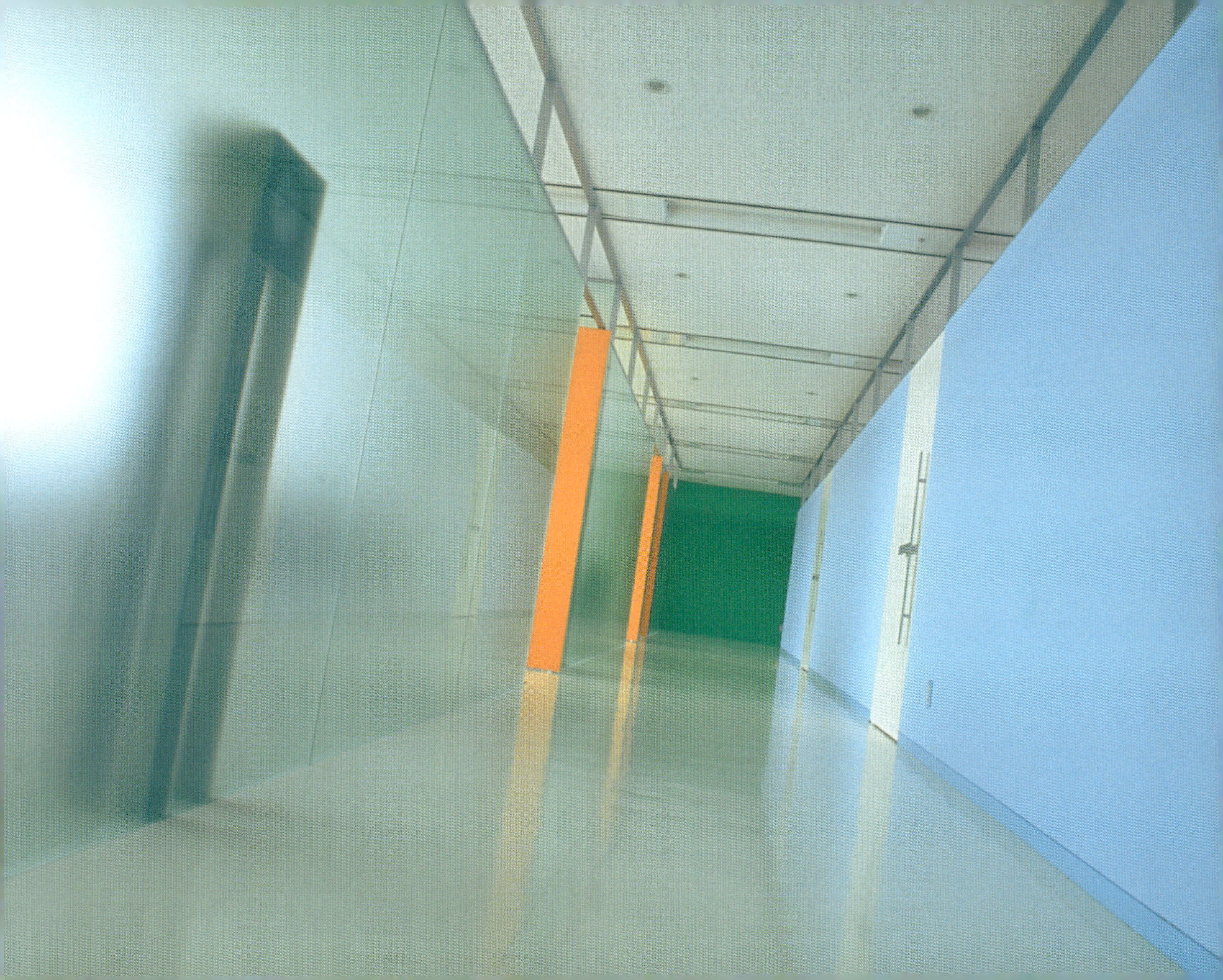

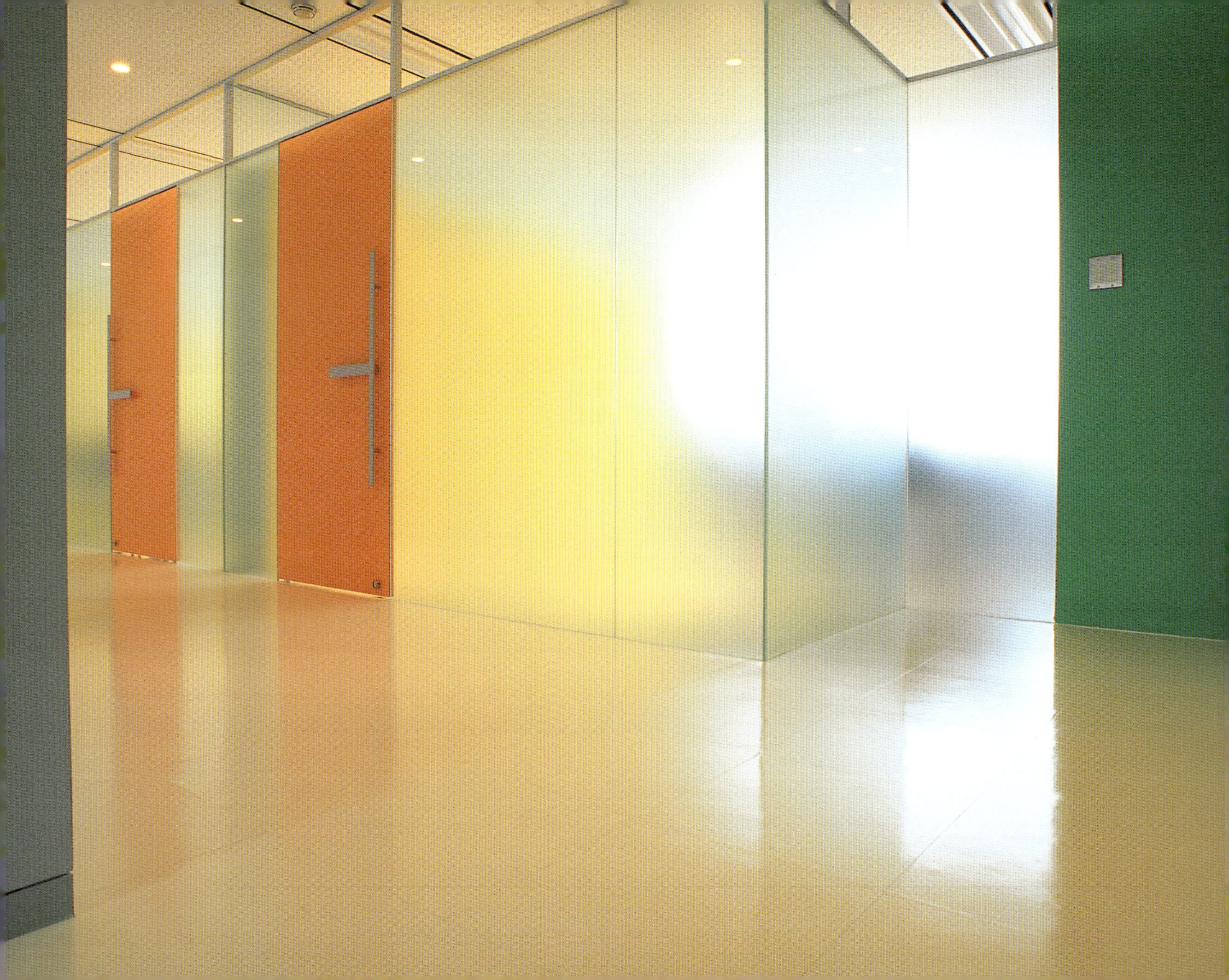

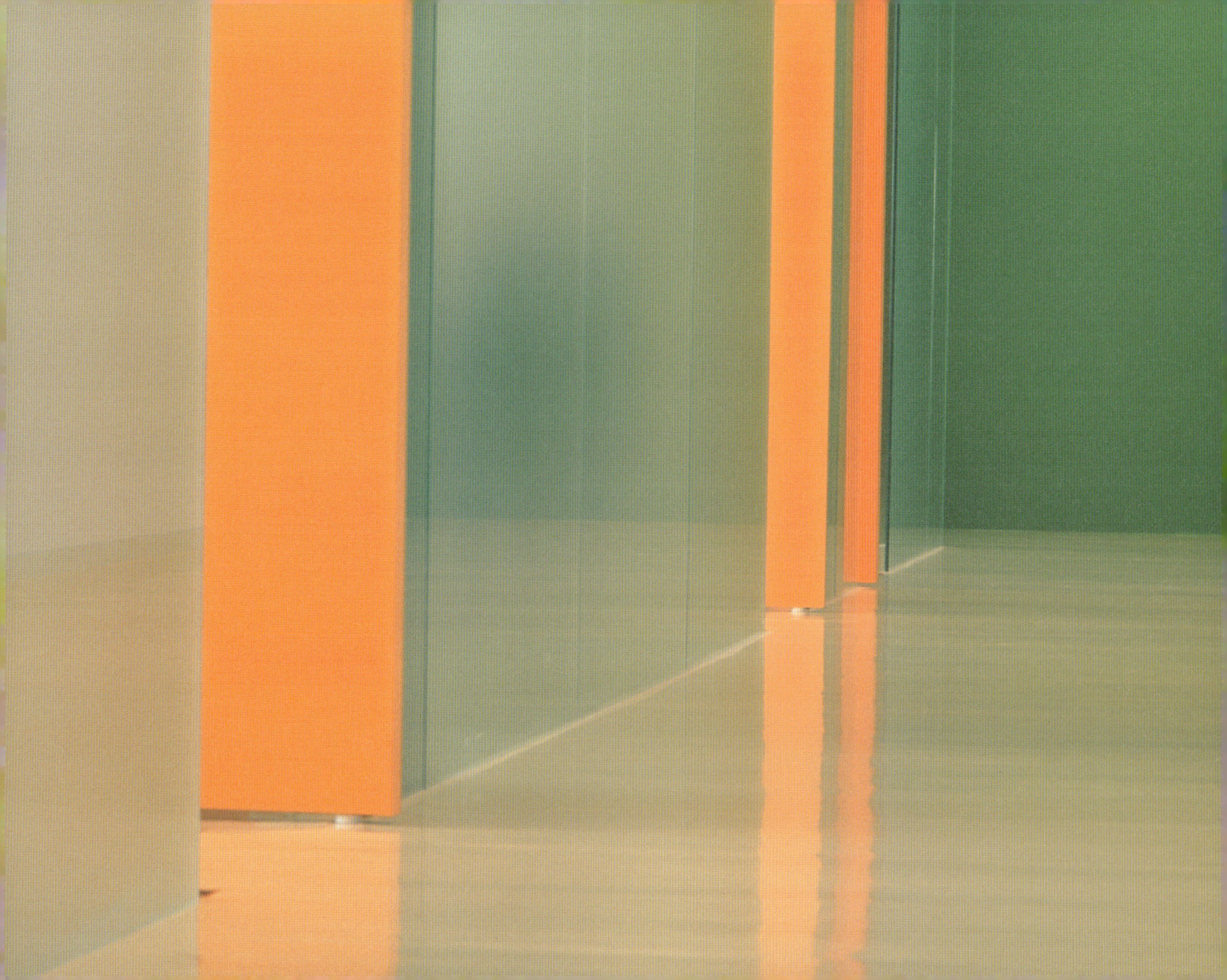

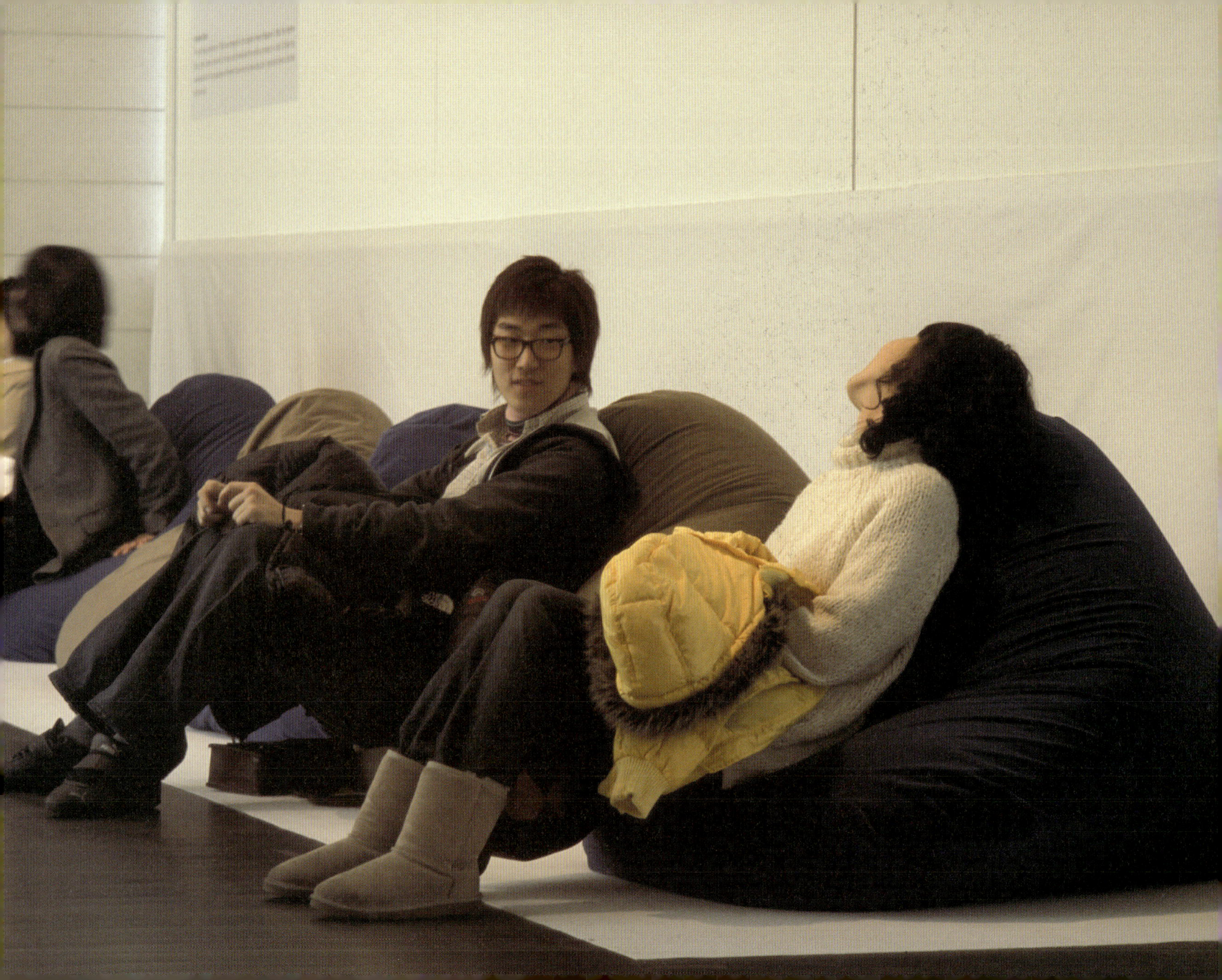

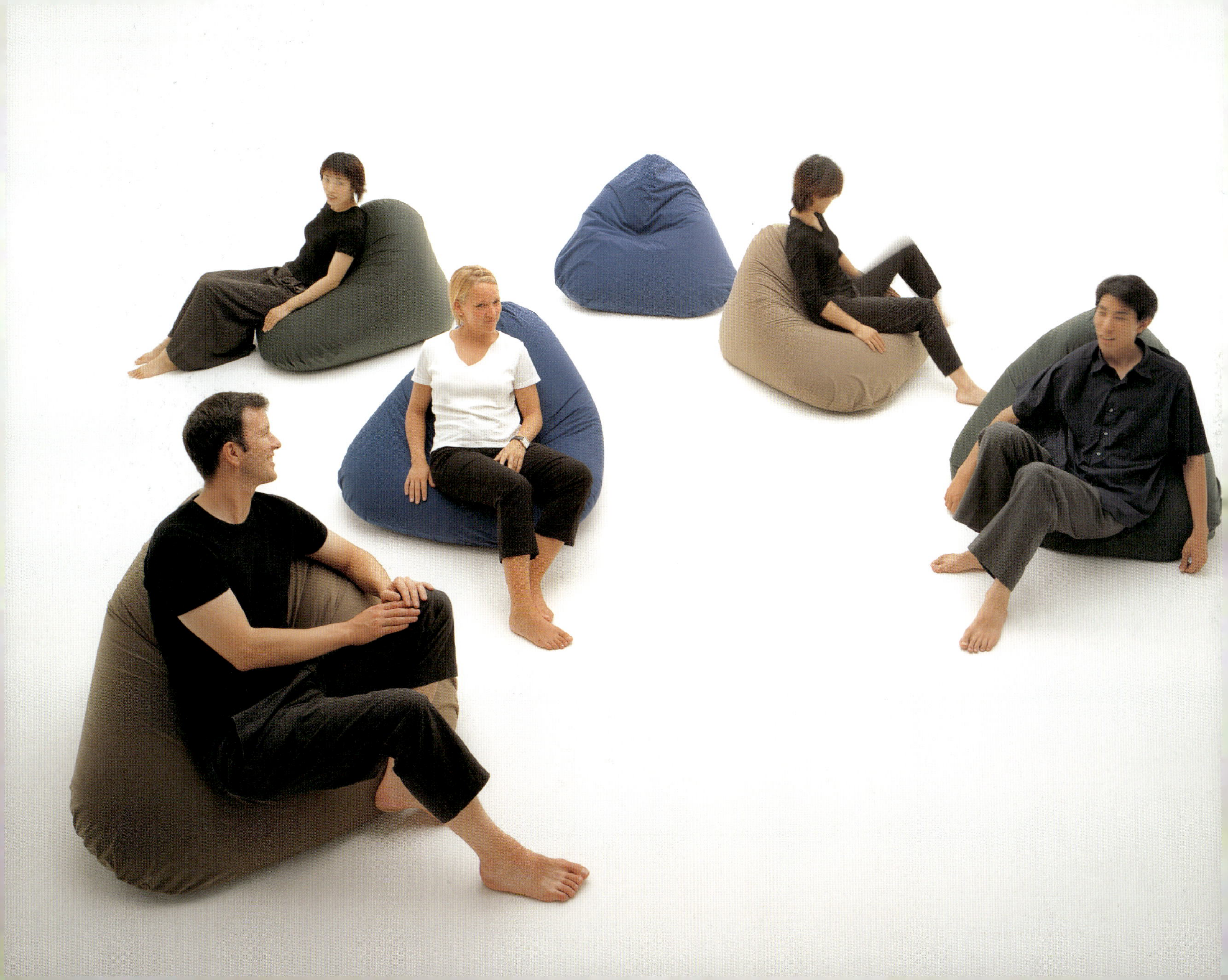

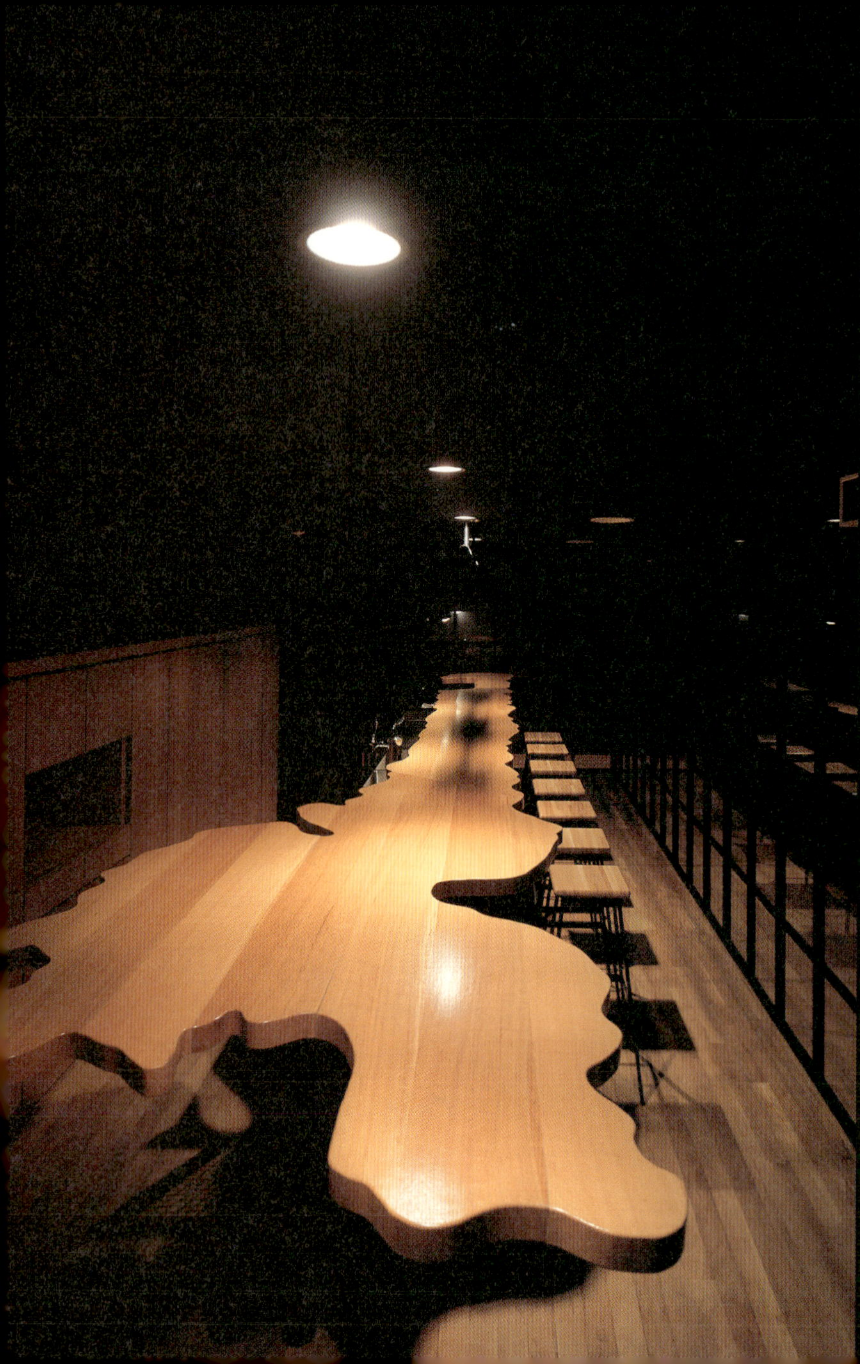

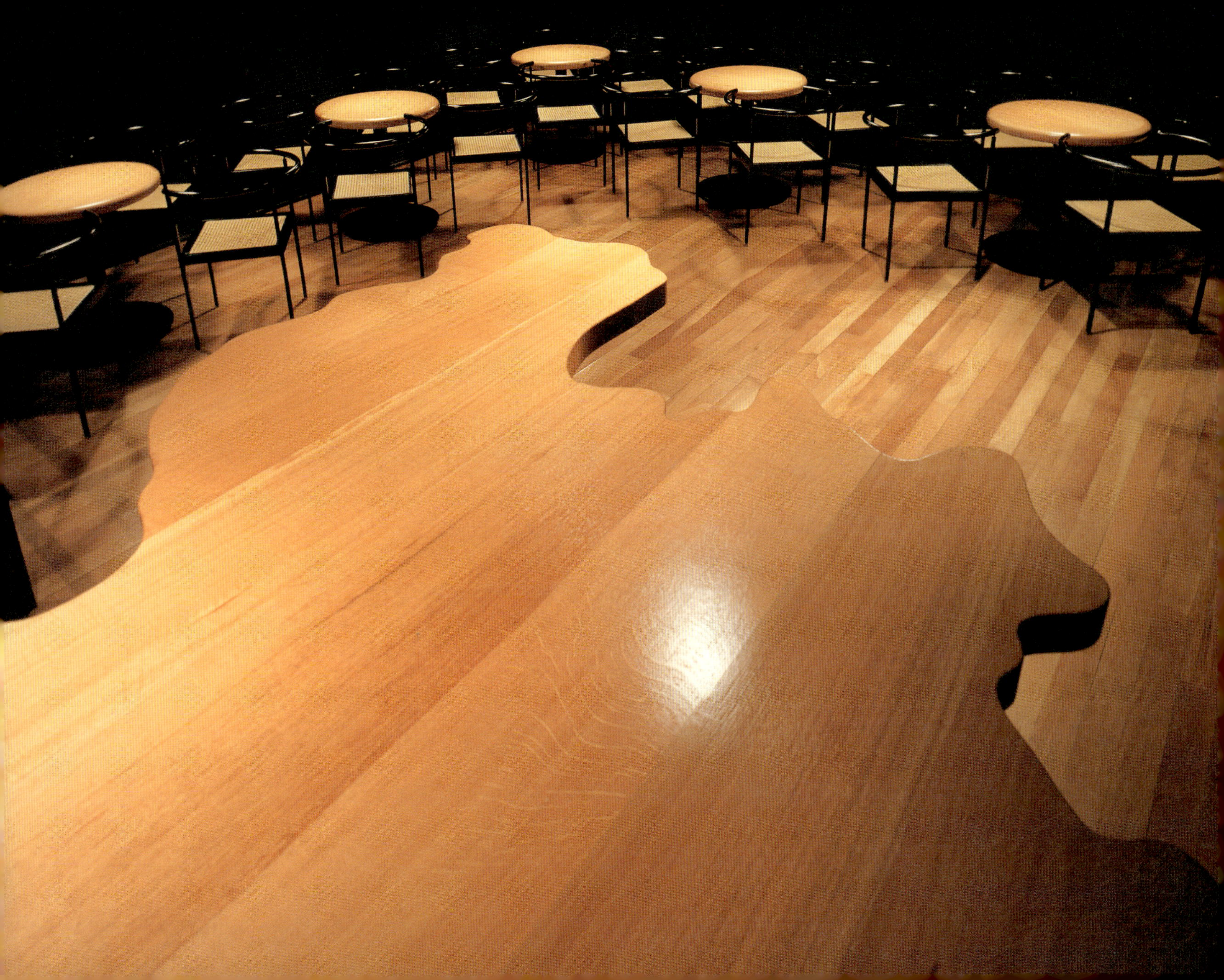

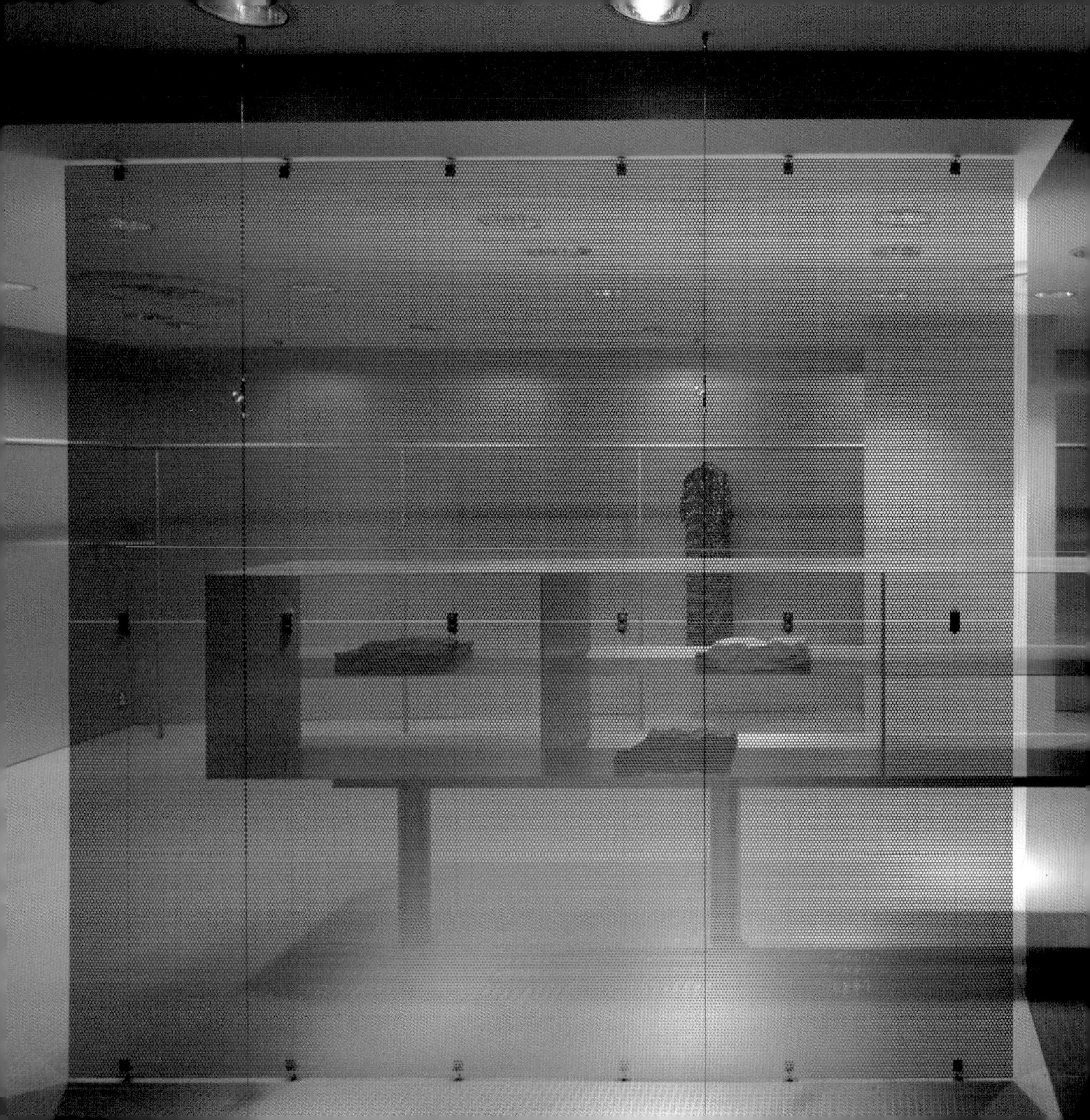

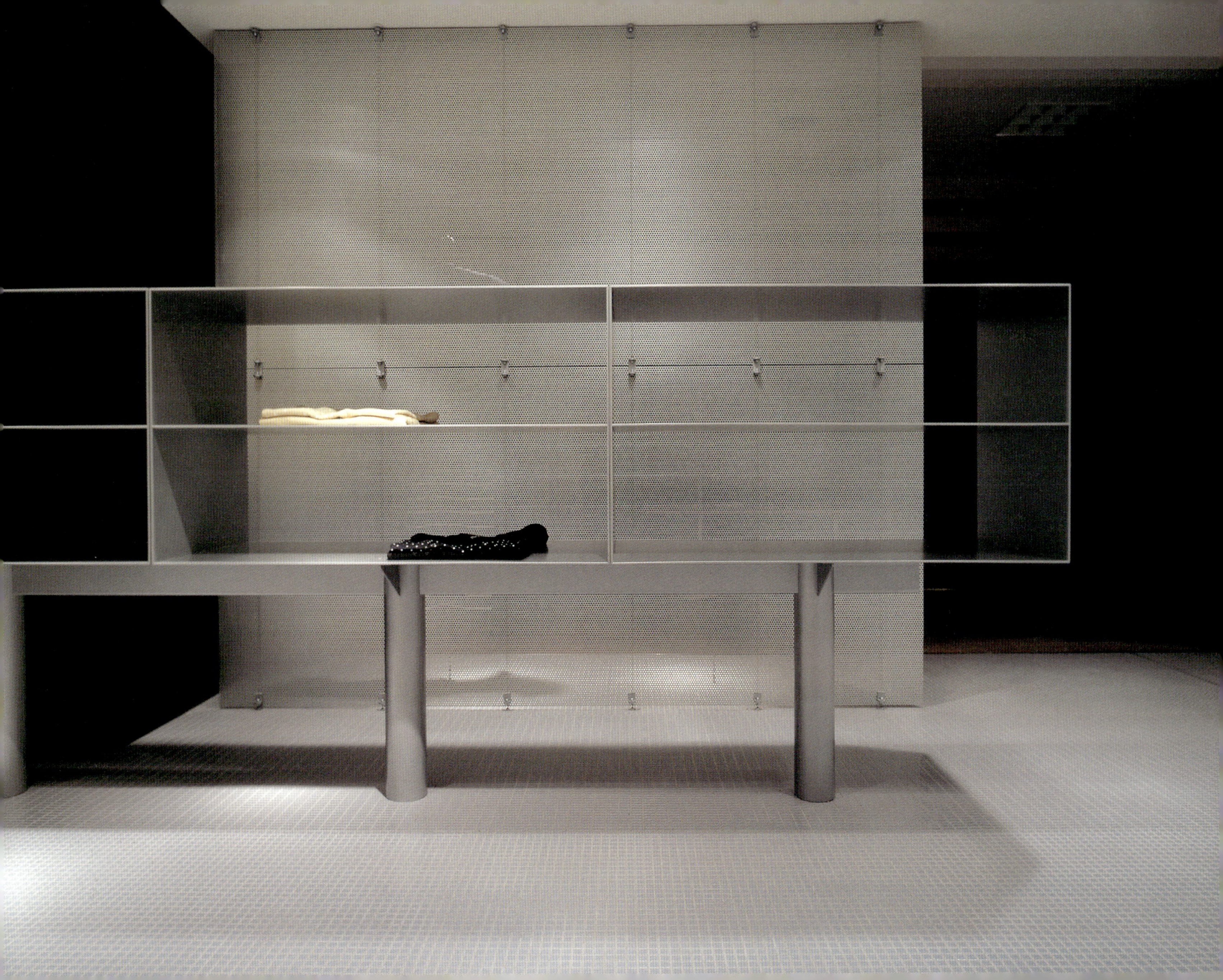

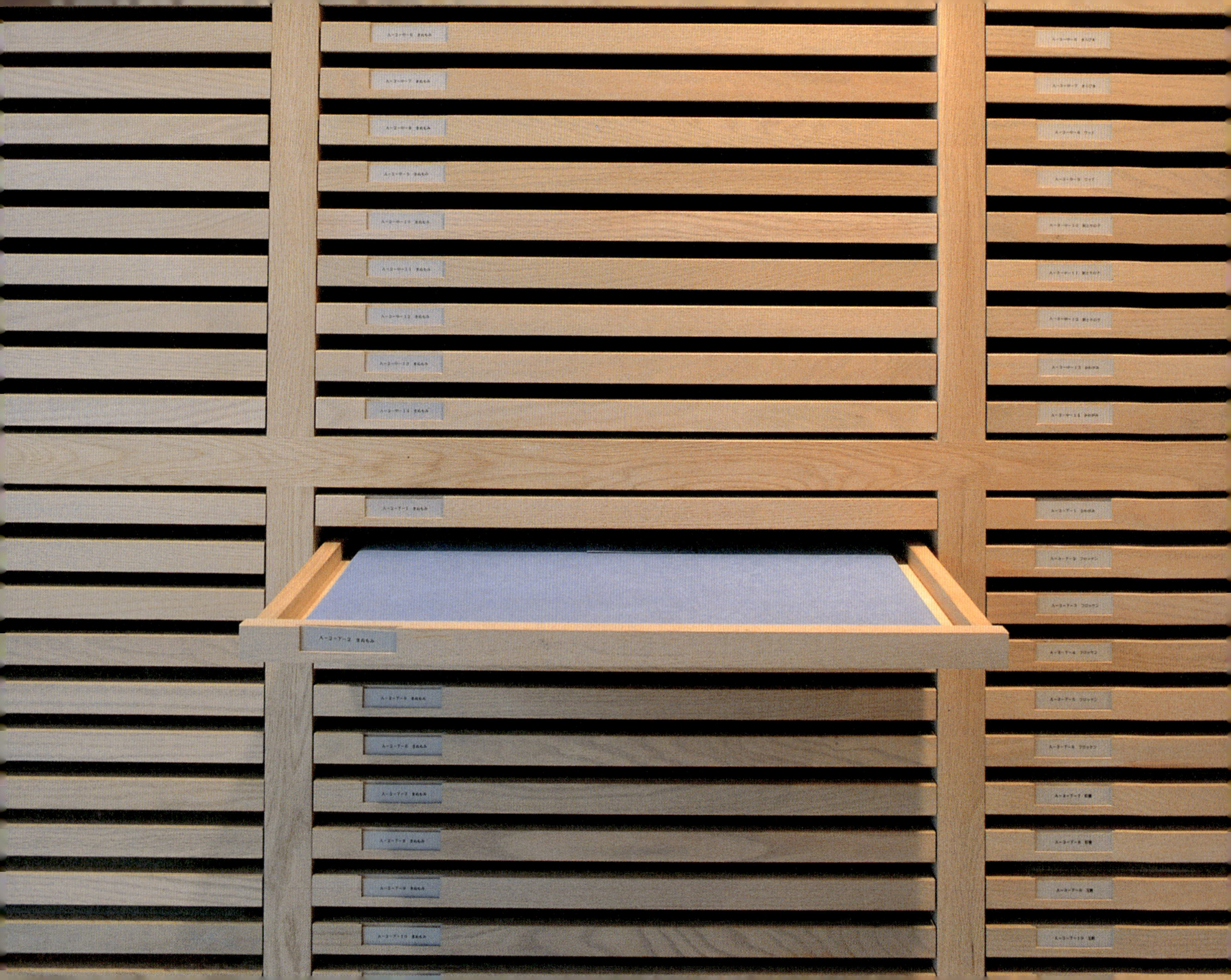

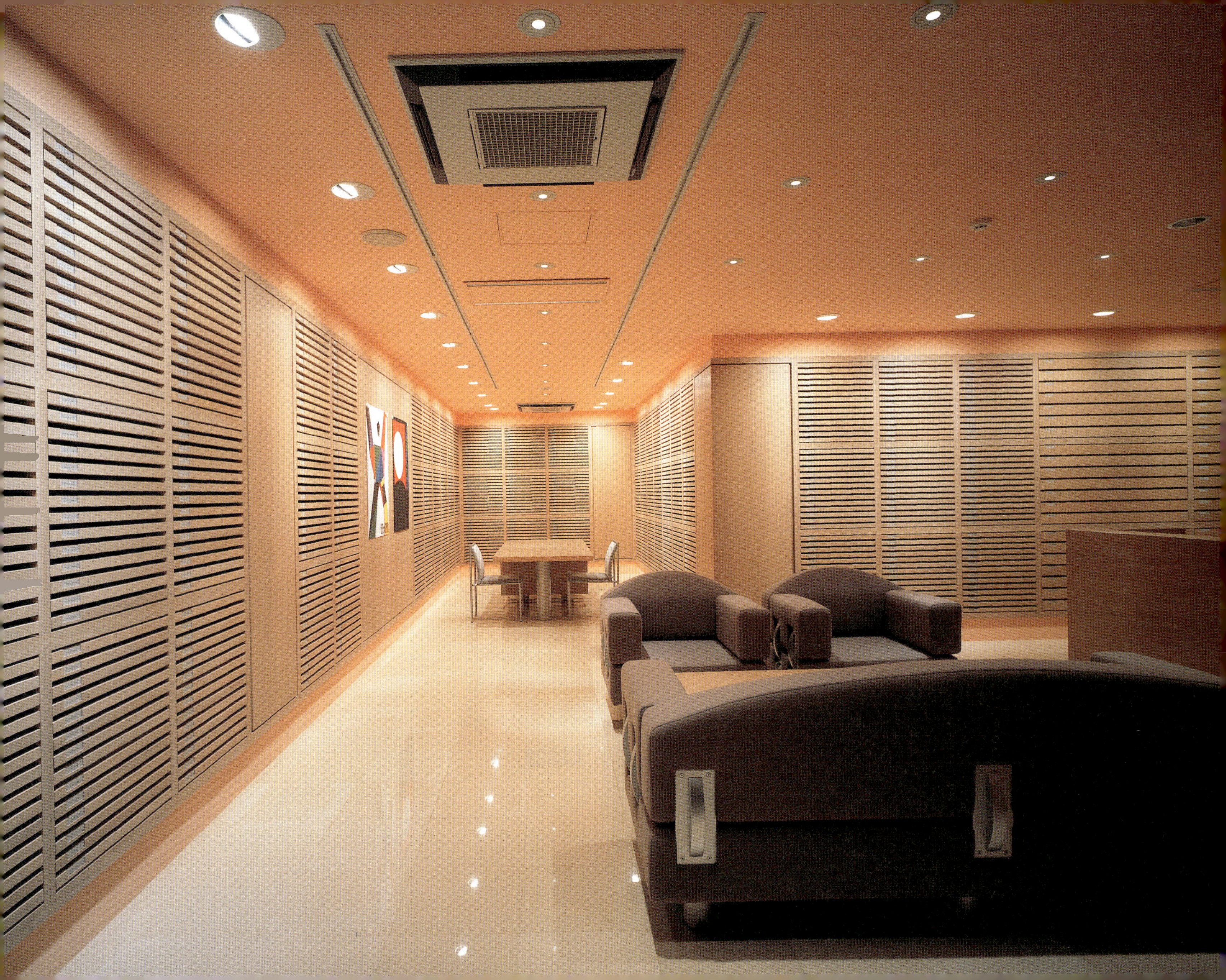

МРАТ

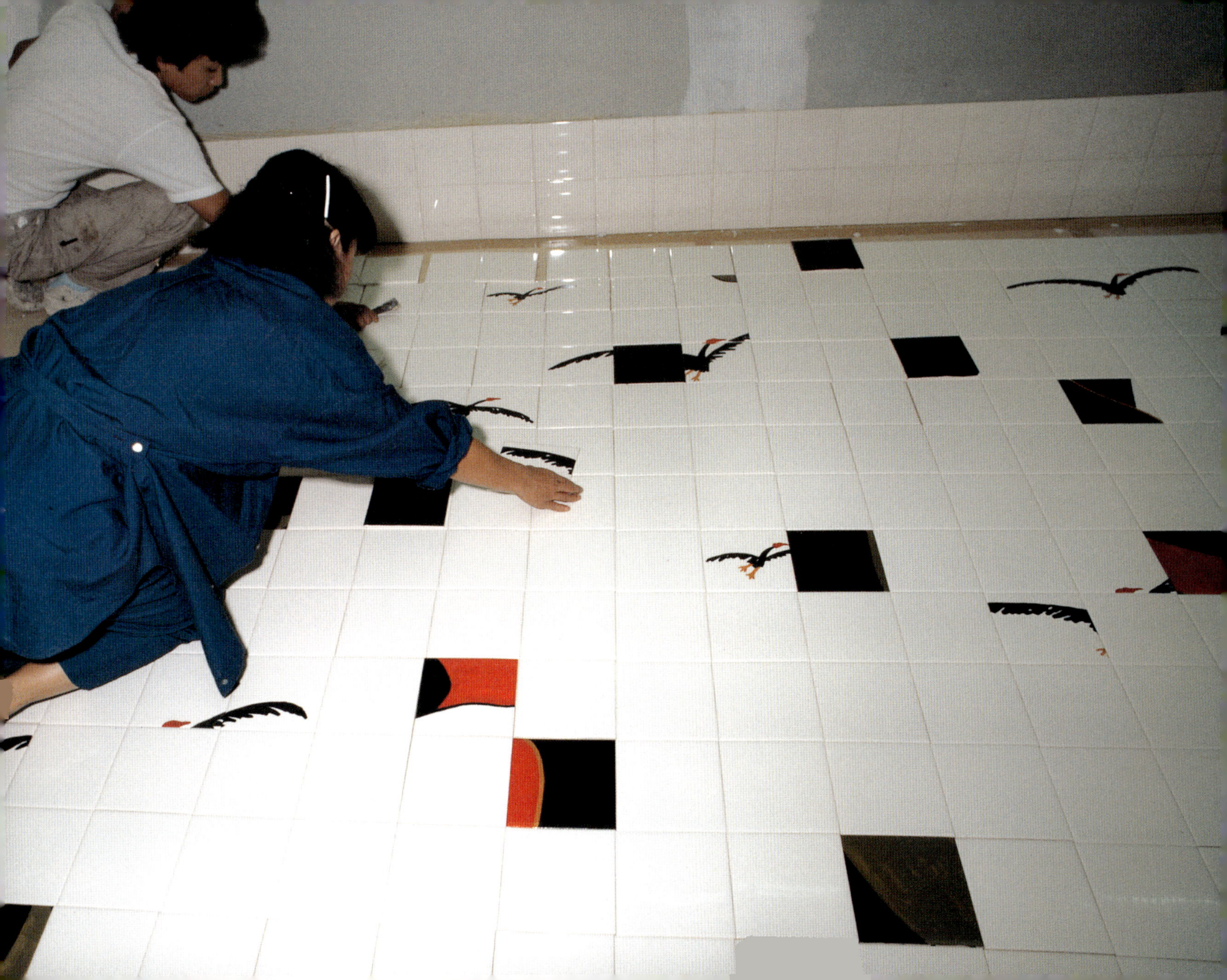

木蘭
Mu Lan

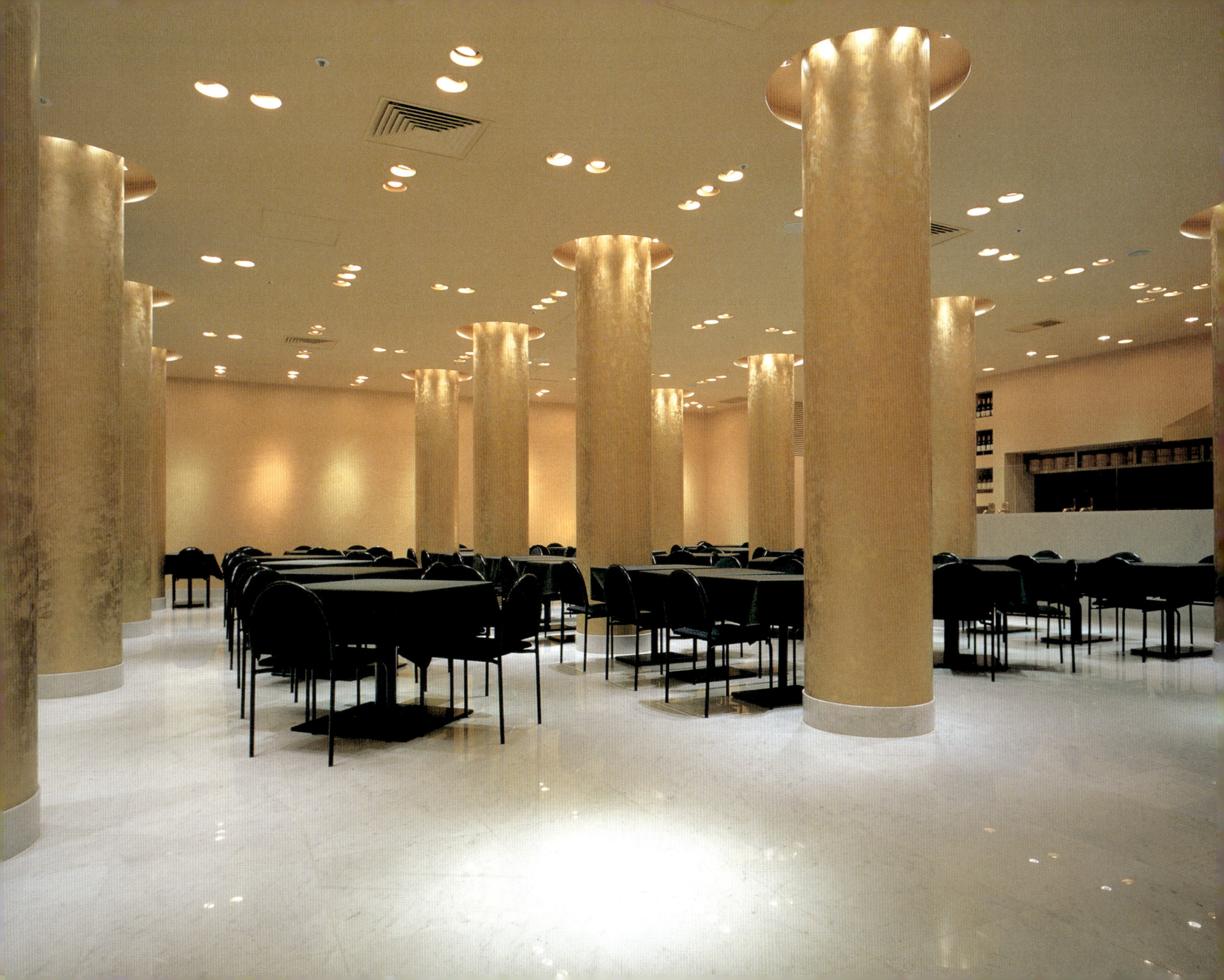

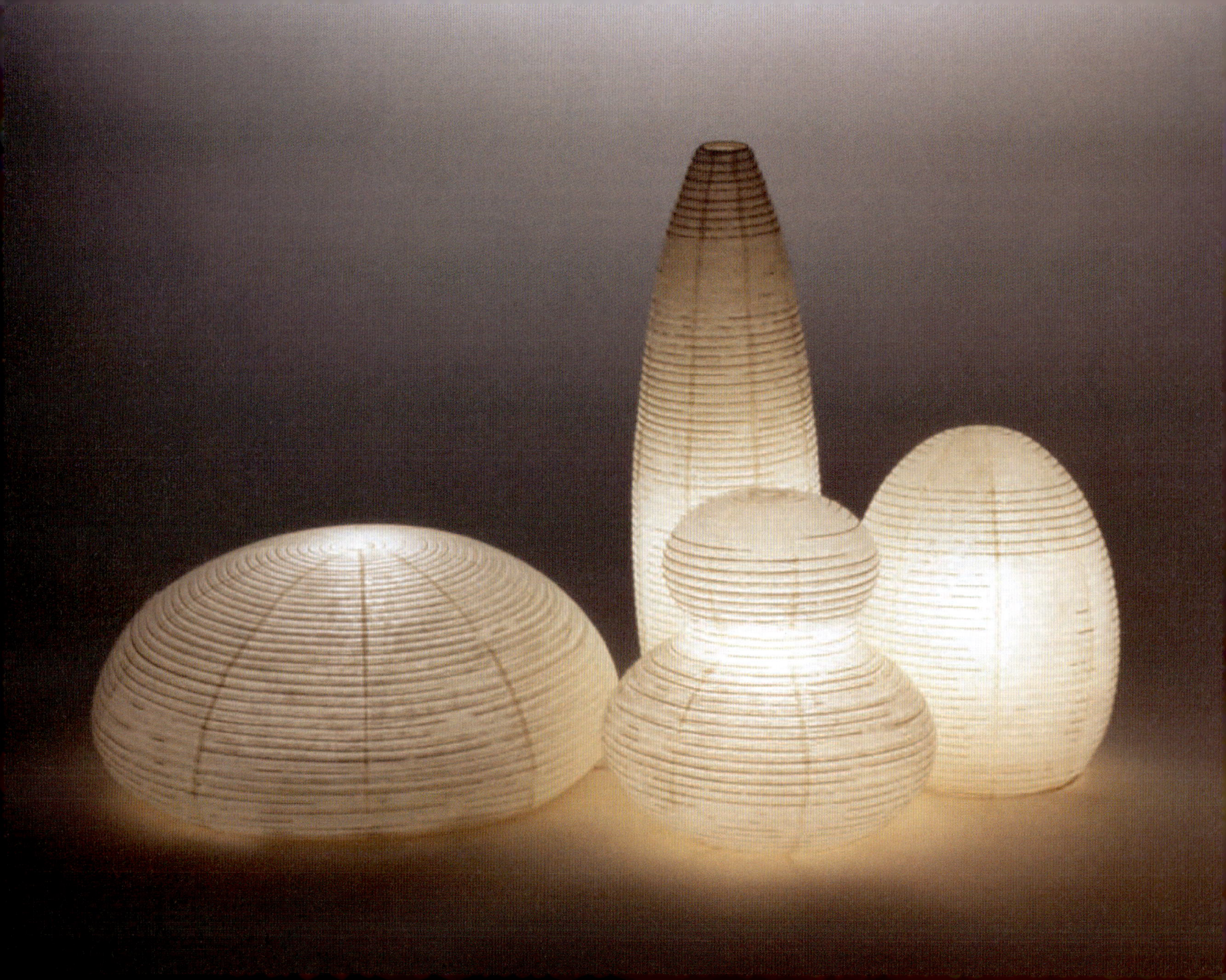

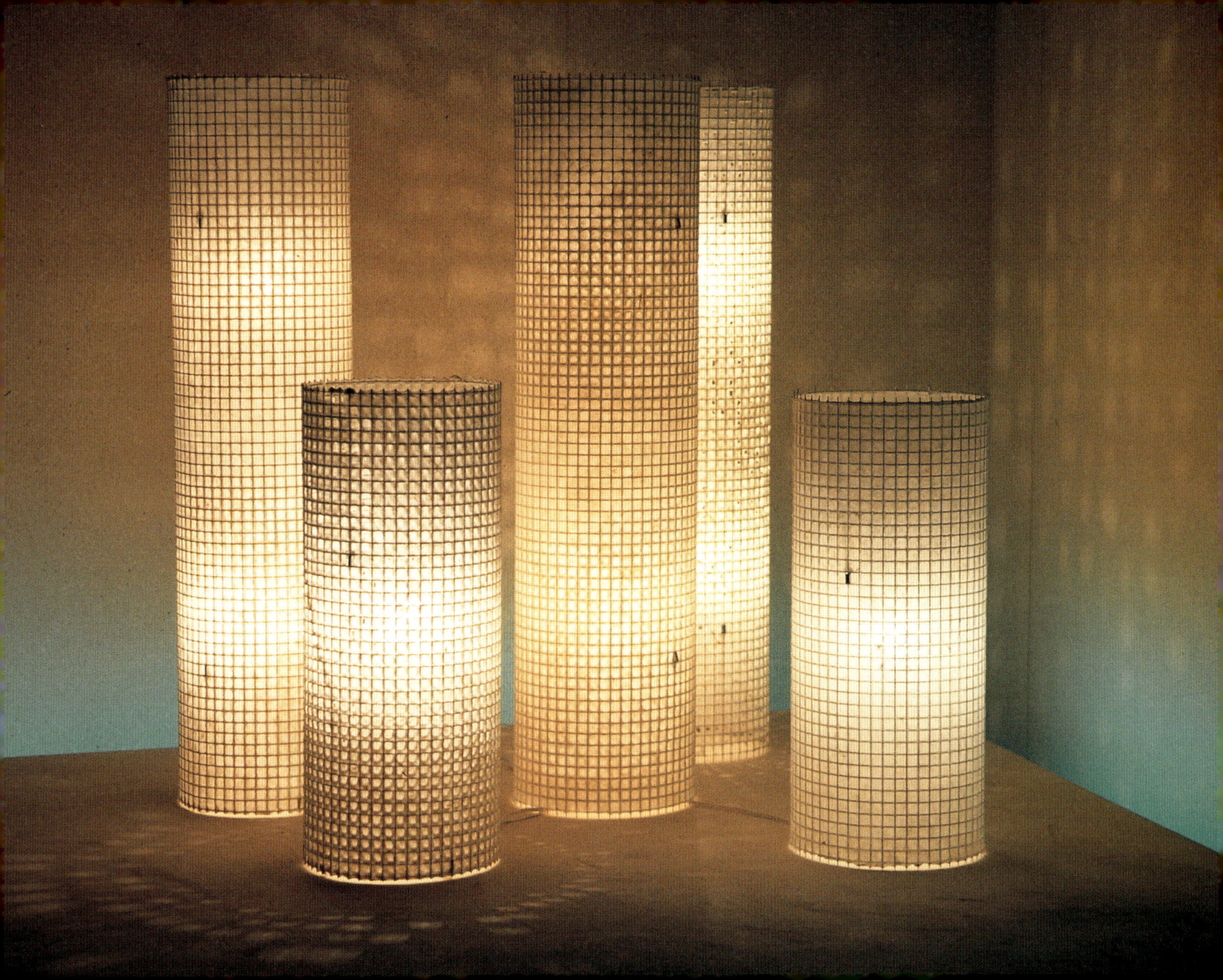

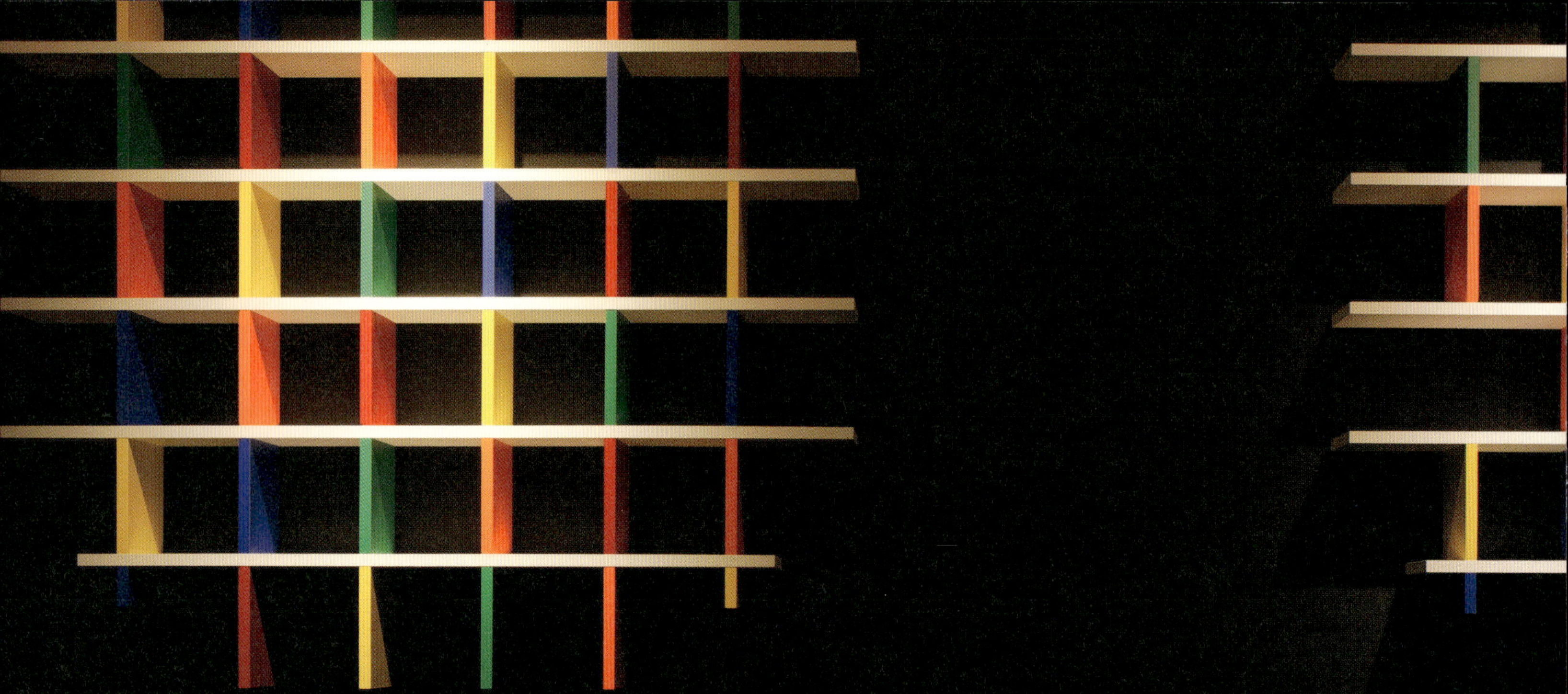

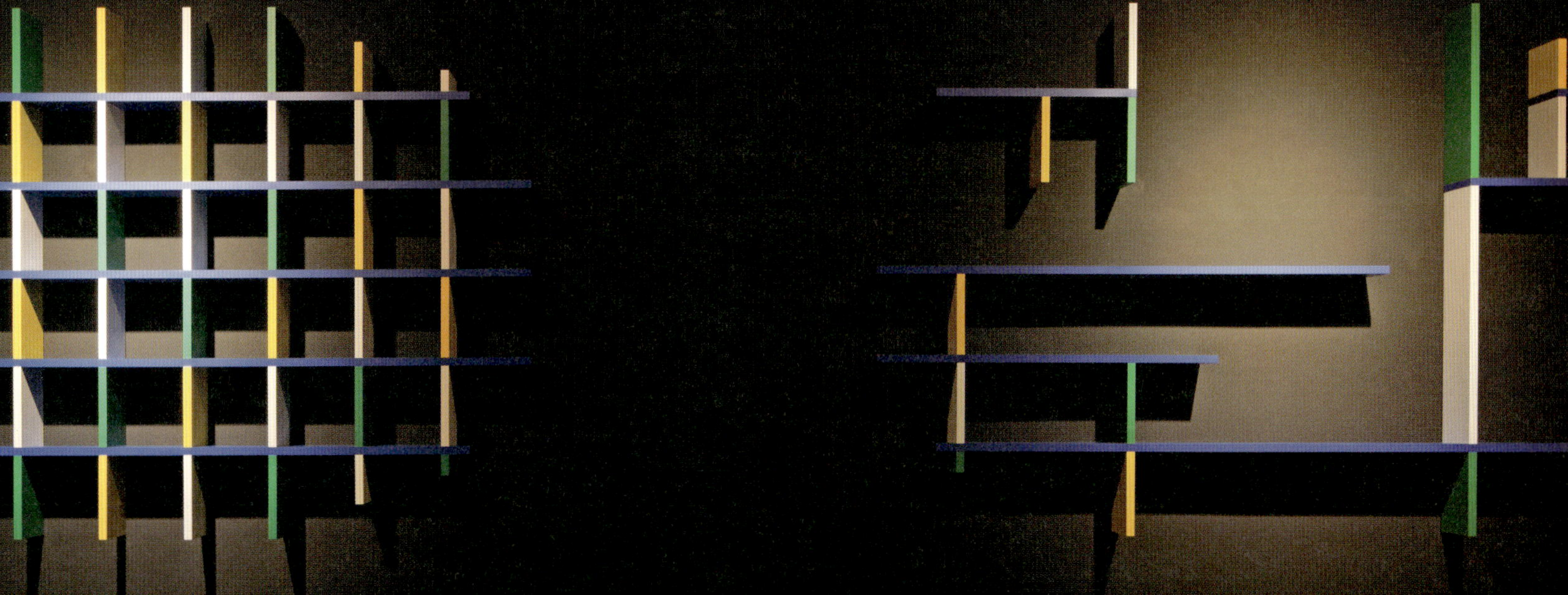

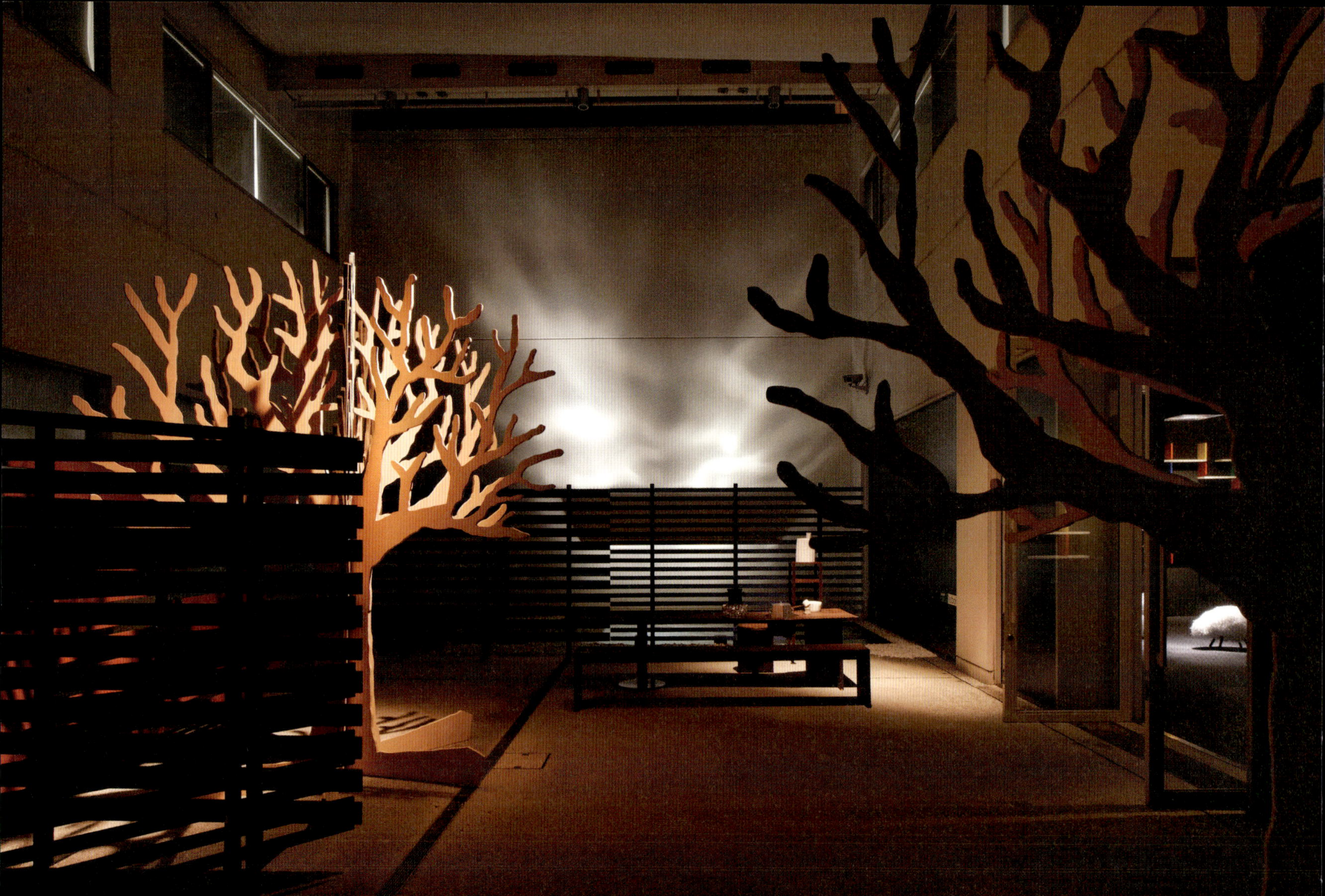

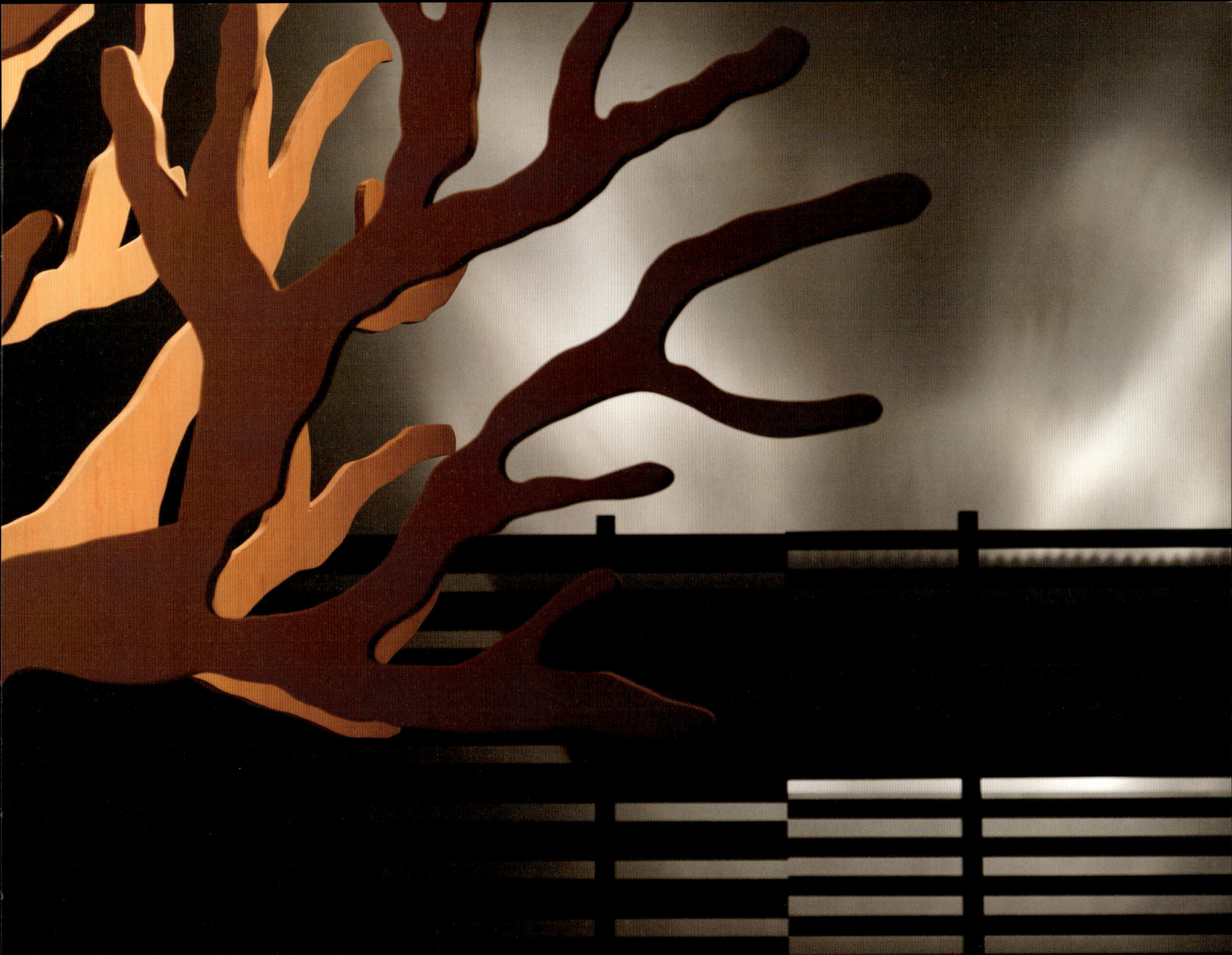

弱さという感覚世界のデザイン
……ぼやけたもの　霞んだもの　透けたもの　ゆらいだもの

　美的世界において［弱さ］は独特のニュアンスをつくり出します。繊細で一見壊れやすいもの、小さくて細やかなもの、柔らかくて不定形なものには、硬くて丈夫で大きなものには見られない独特のものがあります。

　また、見えない何かを想い、静かにたたずむ描写には、人の気持ちにやさしさと静けさ、危うさと切なさをつくり出します。

　これらの弱さとは、けして強さとの対比ではなく、弱さが独自にもつ特性です。

　［弱さ］は、今日社会において排除の対象でした。曖昧で不確かなものは不安定さといった点において排除され、移ろいやすくゆらいだものは、計りにくいものとして理解の外におかれました。

　しかし、実際の自然や人間を取り巻く現象は予測不可能なものであり、けして確定的なものでもなく、移りやすく気まぐれです。それは今という瞬間の世界、日々刻々と変わる日常の世界は、束の間の世界の連続の上に成り立っているからです。

　ここに挙げた、ぼやけたもの、霞んだもの、透けたもの、ゆらいだもの、という言葉が表す状況は、20世紀社会がもっとも嫌った現象でした。しかし、この言葉のなかに人の心と深く関わる何かが含まれています。

　この本を通して多くの方々に考えていただくきっかけになれば幸いです。

　最後に、長年私の作品を撮影してくださった淺川敏さん、ナカサ＆パートナーズのみなさん、平井広行さん、白鳥美雄さん、この本を編集してくださった工作舎の米澤敬さんに感謝します。

内田繁

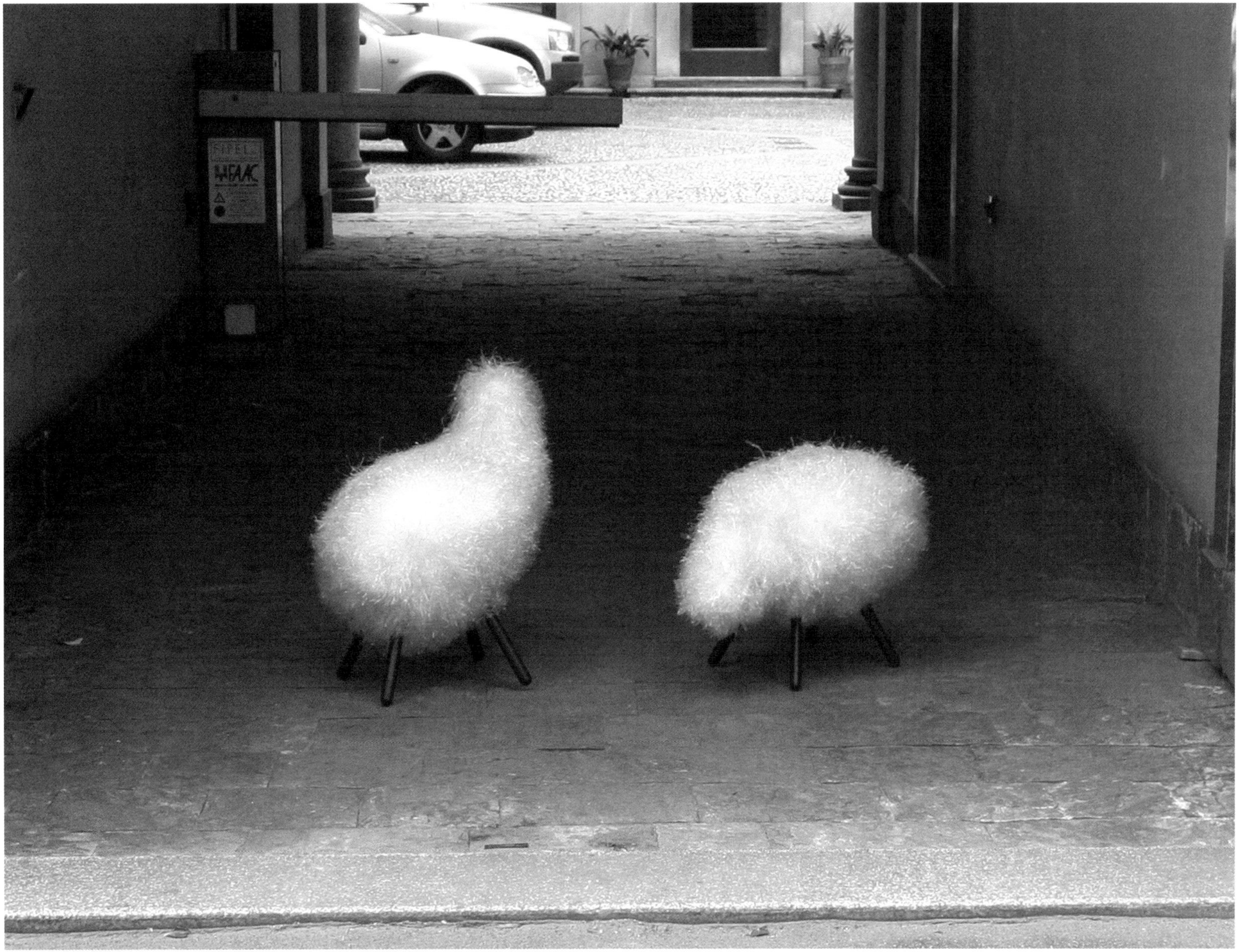

A world of design based on a sense of weakness
—— Vague, hazy, transparent, wavering things

In the world of esthetics, "weakness" has a very peculiar nuance. Delicate and seemingly fragile things, small and modest things, soft and irregular things all have a certain quality that you do not find in big, strong and sturdy things.

Thinking about something that cannot be seen and quietly trying to portray it creates a mood of gentleness, serenity, precariousness and longing.

These kinds of weakness are by no means in opposition to strength; they are characteristics that only belong to weakness.

In today's world, "weakness" is often considered something that ought to be eliminated.

Ambiguous and indefinite things are abolished as being insecure. The transient and flickering is excluded from understanding because it is difficult to measure.

However, nature and the real world that surrounds us is full of unpredictable phenomena. Far from being stable, it is ever-changing and capricious. That is because the world of "right now," the world that changes day by day, hour by hour, is made up of a succession of fleeting moments.

The conditions described by the words I mentioned in the heading – "vague, hazy, transparent, wavering things" – were the phenomena that the 20th century loathed the most. However, something in these words have a profound relationship with the human mind.

I hope that this book will make many people reflect on these matters.

Finally, I would like to express my gratitude to Satoshi Asakawa, who has photographed my work over many years, the staff of Nacàsa & Partners Inc., Hiroyuki Hirai and Yoshio Shiratori, and last but not least Kei Yonezawa of Kousakusha, who edited this book.

Shigeru Uchida

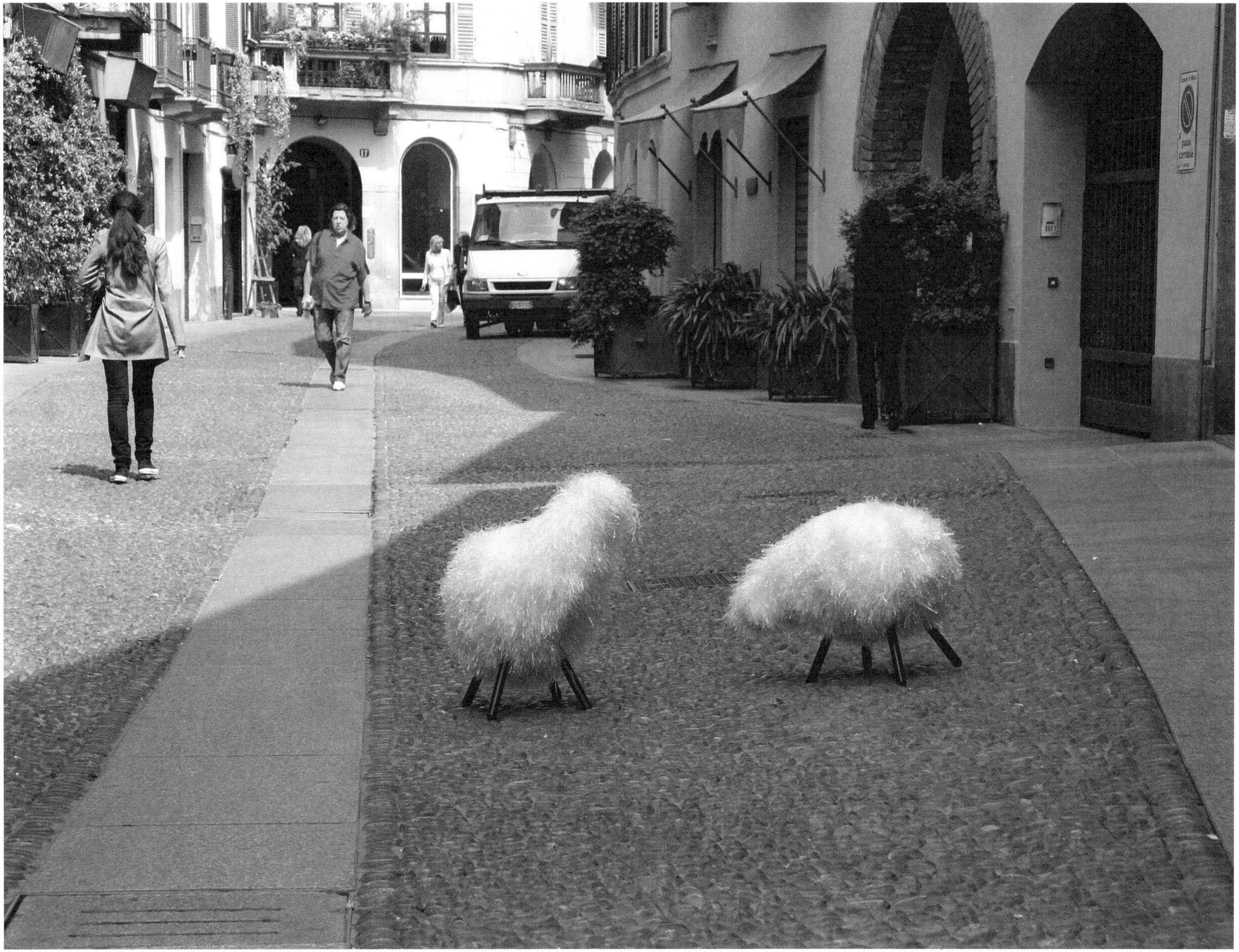

INDEX

Right: Dancing Water / 2007 / Sense of Weakness in Design (Milan・2007) / ○

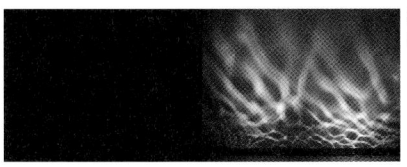

Right: Dancing Water / 2007 / Sense of Weakness in Design (Milan・2007) / ◎

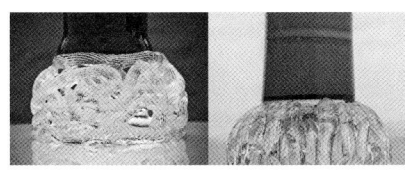

Left: Yaburebukuro（破袋）/ 2006 / Shigeru Uchida Design Exhibition (Seoul・2006) / ■
Right: Vase with bamboo root（竹根付花入）/ 2006 / ■

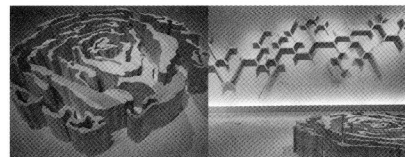

Left: Cabbage / 2008 / How did life begin? – Water, Plants, Life Exhibition（水・植物・生命展）(Tokyo・2008) / ■
Right: Vine / 2008 / How did life begin? – Water, Plants, Life Exhibition（水・植物・生命展）(Tokyo・2008) / ■

Left: Alfie / 2003 / Shigeru Uchida Design Exhibition (Seoul・2006) / ■
Right: Flower Screen / 2004 / Shigeru Uchida Design Exhibition (Seoul・2006) / ■

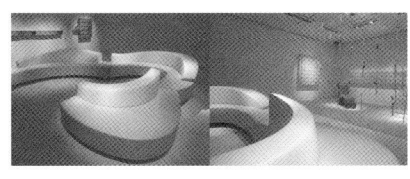

Left: So in Love / 2003 / Shigeru Uchida Design Exhibition (Seoul・2006) / ■
Right: Love, shelf（棚）/ 2003 / Shigeru Uchida Design Exhibition (Seoul・2006) / ■

Left: Shigeru Uchida Design Exhibition (Seoul・2006) / ■
Right: Dengaku / 2004 / Shigeru Uchida Design Exhibition (Seoul・2006) / ■

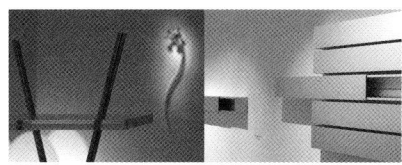

Left: Shigeru Uchida Design Exhibition (Seoul・2006) / ■
Right: Horizontals A-Line / 2003 / Shigeru Uchida Design Exhibition (Seoul・2006) / ■

Left: Shelf（棚）/ 2004 / Shigeru Uchida Design Exhibition (Seoul・2006) / ■
Right: Slender Series（スレンダー・シリーズ）/ 2004 / Shigeru Uchida Design Exhibition (Seoul・2006) / ■

Left: Shigeru Uchida Design Exhibition (Seoul・2006) / ■
Right: Tree / 2001 / Shigeru Uchida Design Exhibition (Seoul・2006) / ■

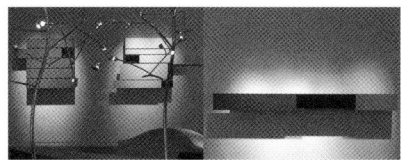

Left: Shigeru Uchida Design Exhibition (Seoul・2006) / ■
Right: Horizontal / 2001 / Shigeru Uchida Design Exhibition (Seoul・2006) / ■

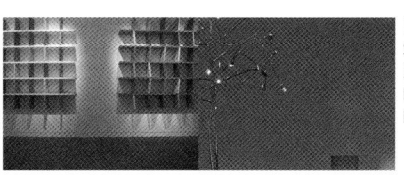

Left: Shelves（棚-01、棚-02）/ 2000 / Shigeru Uchida Design Exhibition (Seoul・2006) / ■
Right: Tree / 2001 / Shigeru Uchida Design Exhibition (Seoul・2006) / ■

INDEX

Left: Okazaki Chair（岡崎の椅子）/ 1996 / Shigeru Uchida Design Exhibition (Seoul・2006) / ■

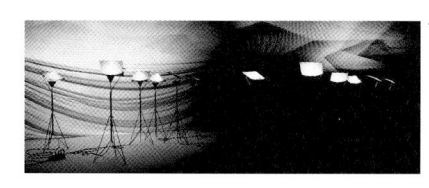

Tenderly / 1986 / Tokyo studio / ●

Left: Shigeru Uchida Design Exhibition (Seoul・2006) / ■
Right: Shigeru Uchida Design Exhibition (Seoul・2006) / ■

"Kimiko By Kimiko" Exhibition (Tokyo・1990) / ◆

Left: Nirvana / 1981 / ▲
Right: Shigeru Uchida Design Exhibition (Seoul・2006) / ■

Left: Dear Vera / 1989 / ■
Right: Pierre Junod watch（腕時計）/ 1995 / ■

Left: NY Chair II / 1986 / Tokyo studio / ●
Right: September / 1977 / Tokyo studio / ●

Left: Dear Fausto / 1989 / Tokyo studio / ●

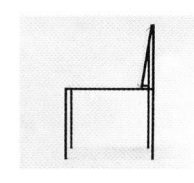

Left: Rattan Chair（籐の椅子）/ 1974 / Tokyo studio / ▲
Right: Shigeru Uchida Design Exhibition (Seoul・2006) / ■

Left: "Ji-an," "So-an" and "Gyo-an" tearooms（茶室「受庵・想庵・行庵」）/ 1993 / Tokyo / ●
Right: "Ji-an" tearoom（茶室「受庵」）/ 1993 / Shigeru Uchida Design Exhibition (Seoul・2006) / ■

Left: Nirvana / 1981 / Shigeru Uchida Design Exhibition (Seoul・2006) / ■
Right: Le Club Roppongi / Tokyo bar / ◆

Left: "Ji-an" tearoom（茶室「受庵」）/ 1993 / Shigeru Uchida Design Exhibition (Seoul・2006) / ■
Right: "Black and White" scroll by Katsumi Asaba; black, cylindrical vase by Keiji Ito（軸「黒と白」（浅葉克己）、黒筒型花入（伊藤慶二））/ Shigeru Uchida Design Exhibition (Seoul・2006) / ■

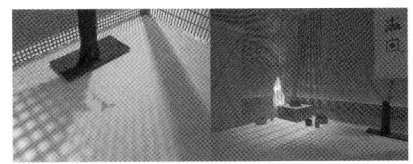

"Ji-an" tearoom（茶室「受庵」）/ 1993 / Shigeru Uchida Design Exhibition (Seoul・2006) / ■

Left: "So-an" tearoom. "Requiem" scroll by Keiji Ito, porcelain vase by Taizo Kuroda（茶室「想庵」、軸「レクイエム」（伊藤慶二）、白磁花入（黒田泰蔵））/ Shigeru Uchida Design Exhibition (Seoul・2006) / ■
Right: "Isotta" water bowl by Bořek Šípek, silver tea caddy by Toru Kaneko, glass tea bowl by Kazumi Tsuiji. porcelain water container by Taizo Kuroda（水指「イゾッタ」（ボジャック・シーペック）、銀格子棗（金子透）、ガラス茶碗（辻和美）、銀茶杓（金子透）、建水・白磁鉢（黒田泰蔵））Shigeru Uchida Design Exhibition (Seoul・2006) / ■

Left: "So-an" tearoom（茶室「想庵」）/ 1993 / Shigeru Uchida Design Exhibition (Seoul・2006) / ■
Right: "So-an" tearoom（茶室「想庵」）/ 1993 / Shigeru Uchida Design Exhibition (Seoul・2006) / ■

Left: "Gyo-an" tearoom. Cylindrical iron pot by Shigeru Uchida, Oribe brazier by Ken Matsuzaki, water bowl by Keiji Ito, lacquer tea container by Toru Matsuzaki, tea bowl with brush strokes by Shiro Tsujimura（茶室「行庵」、円筒釜（内田繁）、織部風炉（松崎健）、水指（伊藤慶二）、朱漆茶入（松崎融）、刷毛目茶碗（辻村史朗））/ Shigeru Uchida Design Exhibition (Seoul・2006) / ■
Right: "Gyo-an" tearoom, "Full Moon" scroll by Katsuhiko Hibino（茶室「行庵」、軸「満月」（日比野克彦））/ Shigeru Uchida Design Exhibition (Seoul・2006) / ■

Left: "Gyo-an" tearoom, vase by Wataru Sato（茶室「行庵」、花入（佐藤亘））/ Shigeru Uchida Design Exhibition (Seoul・2006) / ■
Right: "So-an" tearoom（茶室「想庵」）/ 1993 / Shigeru Uchida Design Exhibition (Seoul・2006) / ■

Left: Table（立礼卓）/ 2002 / Shigeru Uchida Design Exhibition (Seoul・2006) / ■
Right: Table with folding screen by Shunkei Yahagi and square-cut kettle by Shigeru Uchida and Nobuho Miya（立礼卓、四曲一隻屏風（矢萩春恵）、四方切合風炉釜（内田繁・宮伸穂））/ Shigeru Uchida Design Exhibition (Seoul・2006) / ■

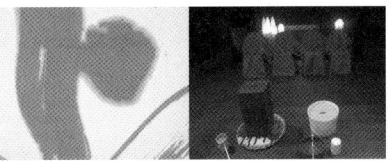

Left: Part of folding screen by Shunkei Yahagi（四曲一隻屏風（矢萩春恵）部分）/ Shigeru Uchida Design Exhibition (Seoul・2006) / ■
Right: Table（立礼卓）/ Shigeru Uchida Design Exhibition (Seoul・2006) / ■

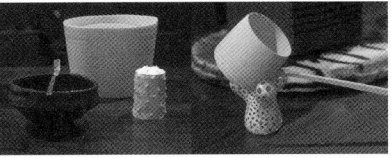

Left: Porcelain water bowl by Taizo Kuroda, silver tea container and tea spoon by Toru Kaneko, black tea bowl by Keiji Ito（白磁水指（黒田泰蔵）、銀茶入（金子透）、黒茶碗（伊藤慶二）、銀茶杓（金子透））/ Shigeru Uchida Design Exhibition (Seoul・2006) / ■
Right: Silver rest by Toru Kaneko（銀蓋置（金子透））/ Shigeru Uchida Design Exhibition (Seoul・2006) / ■

Shigeru Uchida Design Exhibition (Seoul・2006) / ■

INDEX

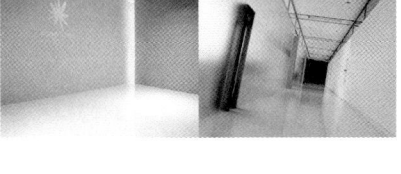

Star Alpha / 2000 / Tokyo office / ■

Star Alpha / 2000 / Tokyo office / ■

Left: Free Form Chair / 1969 / Shigeru Uchida Design Exhibition (Seoul・2006) / ■
Right: Free Form Chair / 1969 / Tokyo studio / ■

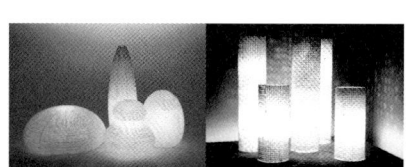

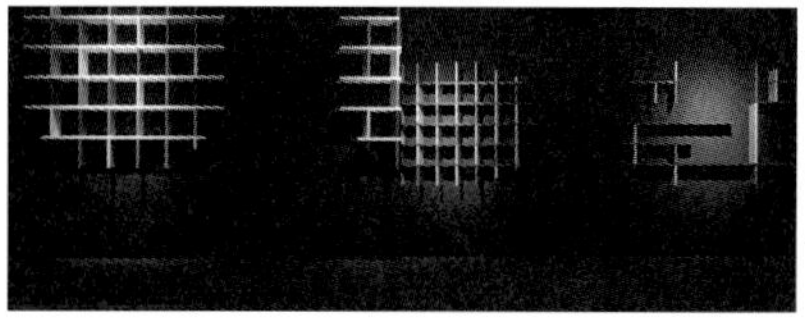

PRONT / 1978 / Tokyo bar / ▲

SUIVI. / 1986 / Tokyo boutique / ●

Left: Aoyama Mihoncho（青山見本帖）/ 1989 / Tokyo showroom / ○
Right: Aoyama Mihoncho（青山見本帖）/ 1989 / Tokyo showroom / ●

MPATA / 1986 / Tokyo boutique / ●

Mulan（木蘭）/ 1999 / Tokyo restaurant / ■

Left: Paper Moon / 2002 / Gifu studio / ○
Right: West of the Moon / 1993 / "Method Remembered" Exhibition (Milan・1995) / ●

Left: A-1, A-2 / 2009 / "Vague, Hazy, Transparent, Wavering" Exhibition (「ぼやけたもの 霞んだもの 透けたもの ゆらいだもの」展) (Tokyo・2009) / ■
Right: B-1、B-2/2009 / "Vague, Hazy, Transparent, Wavering" Exhibition (「ぼやけたもの 霞んだもの 透けたもの ゆらいだもの」展) (Tokyo・2009) / ■

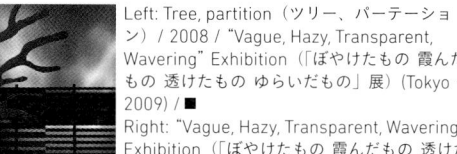

Left: Tree, partition（ツリー、パーテーション）/ 2008 / "Vague, Hazy, Transparent, Wavering" Exhibition (「ぼやけたもの 霞んだもの 透けたもの ゆらいだもの」展) (Tokyo・2009) / ■
Right: "Vague, Hazy, Transparent, Wavering" Exhibition (「ぼやけたもの 霞んだもの 透けたもの ゆらいだもの」展) (Tokyo・2009) / ■

Right: Moo / 2007 / Milan / ○

Right: Moo / 2007 / Milan / ○

Photographs
■ Satoshi Asakawa（淺川 敏）
◆ Hiroyuki Hirai（平井広行）
● Nacàsa & Partners Inc.
▲ Yoshio Shiratori（白鳥美雄）
◎ Shiro Kotake（小竹四郎）
○ Uchida Design Inc.（内田デザイン研究所）

内田 繁 Shigeru Uchida

1943年横浜生まれ。桑沢デザイン研究所所長。毎日デザイン賞、芸術選奨文部大臣賞等受賞。紫綬褒章受章。メトロポリタン美術館（NY）、モントリオール美術館等に永久コレクション多数。日本を代表するデザイナーとして国際的評価を受けるなか、世界各国での講演、国際コンペティションの審査、ミラノ、NY、ソウル等での展覧会、世界のデザイナーの参加するデザイン企画のディレクションなど、つねにその活動が新しい時代の潮流を刺激し続けている。

President of Kuwasawa Design School. He is a recipient of numerous prestigious awards including the Mainichi Design Award and Educations Minister's Art Encouragement Prize. His works are held in permanent collections at the Metropolitan Museum of Art, the San Francisco Museum of Art, the Conran Foundation and others.

Designscape

発行日	2009年10月10日
著者	内田 繁
撮影	淺川 敏＋平井広行＋Nacàsa & Partners Inc.＋白鳥美雄＋小竹四郎＋内田デザイン研究所
翻訳	Jan Fornell
編集	米澤 敬
編集協力	長谷部匡＋佐賀麗菜（内田デザイン研究所）
装幀	松田行正＋相馬敬徳
印刷・製本	文唱堂印刷株式会社
発行者	十川治江
発行	工作舎 editorial corporation for human becoming 〒104-0052 東京都中央区月島 1-14-7-4F phone: 03-3533-7051 fax: 03-3533-7054 URL: http://www.kousakusha.co.jp e-mail: saturn@kousakusha.co.jp ISBN978-4-87502-422-4

Designscape
©2009 by Shigeru Uchida
Japanese edition ©2009 by Kousakusha
Tsukishima 1-14-7, Chuo-ku, Tokyo 104-0052 Japan

好評発売中●工作舎の本

普通のデザイン
内田 繁

刺激的で普通でないものが溢れ続ける現代、日本人は本来の美しさを忘れたのか？
身体感覚や感性を活かした「普通のデザイン」を提唱する。
A5 判変上製／140 頁／定価 本体 1800 円＋税

Ordinary Design
Shigeru UCHIDA

Our cities and living spaces today are overflowing with extreme designs and literally extra-ordinary designs. Have the Japanese forgotten their traditional sense of beauty? In a series of lectures, the world-famous interior designer proposes a 'beautiful design' for the future based on the bodily senses, and a critique of 20th century modernism and the standardization enforced by globalization.

茶室とインテリア
内田 繁

玄関を入ると靴を脱ぎ、床に座りたがる日本人の身体感覚を活かす空間デザインとは？
日本の伝統文化のデザインを通じ、暮らしの将来を描き出す。
A5 判変上製／152 頁／定価 本体 1800 円＋税

Tearooms and Interior Design
Shigeru UCHIDA

A theory of Japanese culture from the viewpoint of architecture and furnishings, by the interior designer Shigeru Uchida (1943-). While interest in traditional Japanese lifestyles is on the rise abroad, they have often been neglected by modern designers in Japan. Here, Uchida reveals the hidden essence of some key concepts of Japanese design with a look towards homes and lifestyles of the future.

ジオメトリック・アート
カスパー・シュワーベ＋石黒敦彦／土肥博至 監修／**杉浦康平** 編・造本

対称性、空間分割するデザイン、組む・結ぶデザイン、動きのデザインなど、
美しく不思議な「幾何学モデル」が満載のヴィジュアルブック。オールカラー。
A4 判変型／230 頁／定価 本体 3900 円＋税

Geometric Art
Caspar SCHWABE, Atsuhiko ISHIGURO, Kouhei SUGIURA

Why do people find beauty in geometric forms in nature? The symmetry of polyhedrons and kaleidoscopes, efficient space-packing and harmonious proportions - from Pythagoras to contemporary nano-level physics, the wonders of the world of geometry are untangled by a Buckminsterfullerian art director and one of Japan's leading graphic designers.

脳科学と芸術
小泉英明 編著

なぜ脳へ物理的ダメージを受けても、芸術的表現を損なわないのか。認知科学や
脳神経科学の最新成果と、アーティストの体験的考察から、脳と芸術の不思議に迫る。
A5 判上製／424 頁／定価 本体 3800 円＋税

Brain Science & the Arts
Hideaki KOIZUMI (ed.)

Why are we - and other animals - attracted to beauty? Why can some aphasic patients still sing? Can artistic expressions be brought about by brain disease?
Researchers at the cutting edge of cognitive science and neurology and experts in rehabilitation and infant development present their latest results, and artists discuss personal experiences that transcend any particular time and locality.

撮る
今村昌平

日本映画界が誇る巨匠、今村昌平。助監督時代から遺作「赤い橋の下のぬるい水」まで、
インタヴュー、エッセイ、スチールで明かすイマムラ映像の全貌。
A5 判上製／360 頁／定価 本体 3200 円＋税

Shooting
Shouhei IMAMURA

Twofold winner of the Palme d'Or at Cannes, Imamura (1926-2006) was one of Japan's most internationally famous film directors. Here he talks about his early days as an assistant to Ozu, gives his opinions on actors and acting, and discusses each of his many films in an engaging, essayistic style. The book also includes plenty of photographs, a complete filmography and other data.

田中泯　海やまのあひだ
岡田正人 写真／**宇野邦一＋松岡正剛＋木幡和枝** 寄稿

ダンサー田中泯と写真家岡田正人の 30 年におよぶコラボレーションの記録。
舞台は東京「夢の島」の泥海から、山梨「桃花村」の岡と森の四季まで。
300×295mm 上製／126 頁／定価 本体 9000 円＋税

Min Tanaka - Between Mountain and Sea
Masato OKADA

For over 30 years the photographer Masato Okada followed the world-famous Butoh dancer, Min Tanaka, trying to capture the invisible essence of his dance: among mountains, in rivers, and perhaps most strikingly, among the rubbish at Tokyo's garbage dump. This gorgeous volume of photographs also contains several essays in both English and Japanese.